THE

FEAST & FETTLE

COOKBOOK

THE
FEAST & FETTLE
COOKBOOK

Unlock the Secret to Better Home Cooking

MAGGIE MULVENA PEARSON

Countryman Press

An Imprint of W. W. Norton & Company
Independent Publishers Since 1923

MAKE IT BETTER

FEAST & FETTLE

For information about permission to reproduce selections
from this book, write to Permissions, Countryman Press,
500 Fifth Avenue, New York, NY 10110

For information about special discounts for bulk purchases, please contact
W. W. Norton Special Sales at specialsales@wwnorton.com or 800-233-4830

Manufacturing by RRD Asia
Book design by Allison Chi
Production manager: Devon Zahn

Countryman Press
www.countrymanpress.com

An imprint of W. W. Norton & Company, Inc.
500 Fifth Avenue, New York, NY 10110
www.wwnorton.com

978-1-68268-896-0

10 9 8 7 6 5 4 3 2 1

To the Feast & Fettle team and our extended community:
This book is dedicated to you.
Without your unwavering support, belief in our
mission, and constant encouragement, these pages
would never have been written.

CONTENTS

* Indicates that the butter, condiment, dressing, sauce, or spice blend is a separate component and can easily be mixed and matched with other recipes.

INTRODUCTION

From a young age, I've felt an undeniable pull toward food and cooking. Some of my earliest memories involve picking blueberries from my vovó's lush blueberry bushes, then watching her turn them into a juicy blueberry pie or a delightful crumb cake.

My childhood fascination made me a constant presence in her kitchen, always eager to assist with any task. Among the twelve grandchildren on my mom's side, I stood out with my unique passion for cooking. I have since inherited many of my vovó's beloved cooking utensils and often reminisce about the lessons she taught me while cooking together.

My grandparents came from a farming background, and they once ran a small dairy farm when their children were little. My vovó had a strong aversion to wasting food, a principle that deeply shaped her cooking. This reverence for ingredients was evident in her dishes, which paid tribute to both what was available and the rhythms of the New England seasons: from abundant sun-ripened fruit pies in the warmer months to robust soups and stews teeming with root vegetables and hearty greens as the weather cooled. Her cooking was never about extravagance, as she didn't embellish much, but it was a testament to simplicity, nourishment, and comfort.

In my early twenties, while finishing up culinary school at Johnson and Wales University, I worked as a nanny and private chef for a family with three young girls. During my four-plus years with them, I became an integral part of their household. Building on that love of cooking instilled from my Vovó, I learned so much about how to feed a busy family, long before starting a family of my own. I developed skills in meal planning, setting early dinner times, managing picky eating, and understanding the importance of exposing children to diverse flavors and textures.

I took these strategies, plus my collection of recipes, and began cooking professionally for other local families, helping them get dinner on the table quickly. It was heartwarming to hear how their children loved eating my vibrant blanched broccoli and green beans, how they were trying new foods, or how they were eager to be involved with the weekly meal-planning process.

One of my favorite tricks for broadening the palates of little ones involves dipping sauces! Introducing unfamiliar foods with familiar dips is fun, piques curiosity in kids and, let's admit it, even some picky adults. It's amazing to see what kids will eat when

there's homemade honey-mustard or BBQ sauce on their plates. This strategy significantly influenced Feast & Fettle's emphasis on incorporating a variety of sauces, dressings, vinaigrettes, and condiments into our dishes. And while this approach works well with kids, these additions also elevate, balance, and add layers of complexity and moisture to nearly any dish.

Cooking for me has always been about community and connection, whether it's making cherished family recipes, feeding my husband and two kids, or sharing a weekend meal with friends and loved ones. Starting my company, Feast & Fettle, was an extension of that feeling for me. The act of sharing meals is one of the most powerful ways humans feel grounded and connected to each other. Through my work, I've had the privilege of offering this experience to many more people than I ever imagined!

In April 2016, I founded Feast & Fettle, a New England–based meal delivery service. It came about after recognizing that there was a genuine need for high-quality, freshly prepared meals hand-delivered right to people's doorsteps. Feast & Fettle began with a single employee other than myself—my childhood best friend, Nicole Nix. She bravely left her corporate role to dive in to this new venture with me. We began by working out of a shared space at a local kitchen incubator, Hope & Main. Fueled by our vision and commitment to white-glove service, I even sold my car to purchase our first delivery van. I was convinced that people deserved more than impersonal meals shipped from large factories. We started with the most modest of beginnings with only eight members, many of whom I had the privilege of serving as personal clients. Over the years that number has evolved into a thriving community of thousands of dedicated members.

From the beginning, I understood the need to creatively elevate everyday cooking. Our members eat Feast & Fettle meals multiple times per week, so our dishes must strike the right balance between being familiar and expertly crafted. I aimed to offer menu items such as pulled chicken enchiladas, grilled flank steak, and broiled teriyaki salmon—comforting, homey dishes that make you feel good. But what sets a homemade or restaurant dish apart, making it taste truly spectacular and delicious? The answer is expert seasoning, and, just like it had in my work as a private chef, that became my method for elevating ordinary recipes. At Feast & Fettle, we are known for our delicious salad dressings and vinaigrettes, robust marinades, savory sauces, luscious compound butters, zesty dips, and aromatic spice blends—all of which sit under the umbrella of seasoning. Each of these elements adds complexity to our dishes, making them feel special and beyond ordinary. While preparing sauces, dressings, marinades, and spice blends at home might seem intimidating at first, they really do not require much additional effort. Plus, it's incredibly rewarding. Understanding the nuances of seasoning is often the key to better home cooking, and through this book I'll share with you the techniques and flavors that I've learned along the way.

HOW TO SEASON FOOD

Proper seasoning makes food taste better. It is that simple. However, knowing how to season well is an acquired skill that takes some time, patience, and practice to master. Eventually this skill will become second nature, and before you know it your cooking skills will have vastly improved.

Seasoning is simply adding an ingredient to food to enhance its flavor. There are several ways to season food, but perhaps the most fundamental of all is the addition of salt. Nothing will dramatically improve your cooking skills more than learning how to properly salt food.

As humans, our bodies need sodium chloride—aka salt—to perform vital bodily functions. Therefore, we innately recognize salty as one of the five basic tastes, along with sweet, sour, bitter, and umami (savory) thanks to specific taste receptors. When adding salt to a dish, the food itself doesn't just register to us as salty—the salt is actually working to bring out a variety of complex flavors within the ingredients. Due to its chemical properties, salt can uniquely amplify desired flavors as well as diminish undesired ones. This aspect is noticeable with bitterness, as sodium ions actively suppress the bitter flavor compounds and intensify the sweeter ones, which is why we always add a little salt to chocolate desserts.

Salt also plays a key role in making meat juicier and tastier. When you salt raw meat, liquid from inside is drawn to the surface. The salt dissolves in that liquid and is then reabsorbed by the meat. This technique is referred to as dry brining. I generally prefer this technique over wet brining, as dry brining results in well-seasoned, juicy meat without the risk of flavor dilution from a liquid brine. And you don't have to cram a large container of liquid in your refrigerator! When first starting out with this method, it is helpful to remember the ratio 1:1. For example, to evenly season 1 pound of raw meat, sprinkle 1 teaspoon of kosher salt from a height of at least 5 to 6 inches for uniform distribution.

TYPES OF SALT

For the purpose of this book, let's get familiar with four types of salt:

TABLE SALT (IODIZED): refined, superfine rock salt, which is found in most salt shakers. In the United States, it is often fortified with iodine as a means to prevent iodine deficiency. I do not recommend cooking with table salt, as it can have a somewhat metallic aftertaste. Moreover, because of its superfine texture, it is tricky to work with and can easily lead to oversalting food (case in point: 1 teaspoon of table salt weighs almost twice as much as 1 teaspoon of kosher salt).

KOSHER SALT: gets its name from the traditional Jewish process of koshering meat. In my opinion, kosher salt is the best all-purpose kitchen salt. Chefs love to use this salt because of its pleasant texture and noticeably larger crystals. It is easy to hold in your hand, pinch, and sprinkle evenly over food. Diamond Crystal and Morton are the two prominent brands of kosher salt in the United States. My strong preference is Diamond Crystal—it's what we exclusively use in Feast & Fettle kitchens—because its lighter crystals stick to food better, dissolve quicker, and is less salty by volume. Morton has a more cubic shape, is heavier and denser, and is therefore saltier.

FINE/COARSE SEA SALT: salt made from evaporated seawater. This salt is available as larger standard crystals or as fine crystals that have a sand-like texture. It is industrially made, widely available, and advertised as a healthier option because it contains trace minerals.

FLAKY SEA SALT: salt made from evaporated seawater. This salt is labor intensive to produce and therefore is more expensive to buy. It is great to use as a finishing salt due to its suburb crunch and beautiful crystal structure. It is a delicious way to complete a dish

such as blanched vegetables, grilled fish or steak, and chocolate chip cookies! Popular brands of this salt are Maldon Sea Salt, Celtic Sea Salt, and Jacobsen Salt Co.

GUIDELINES FOR USING SALT

In addition to salt's powerful impact on flavor, it also affects the protein structure of certain foods and can speed up the cooking process. It is also important to recognize that how much salt to use in your cooking is highly dependent on your personal preferences and taste. With that said, make sure to taste food at different intervals while cooking to check on the seasoning.

To maximize salt's capability, here are some guidelines to follow when salting food:

MEAT: Any meat that requires long cooking times such as a roast chicken or braised pork shoulder benefits greatly from seasoning well in advance, about 24 hours. The meat will absorb the salt slowly over time, resulting in superb seasoning throughout. Meat that is going to be grilled or seared, such as chicken breast or steak, can be seasoned right before cooking. This will create a deeply seasoned, browned crust. Alternatively, you can salt your meat as soon as you get home from the market or grocery store, wrap it back up, and let it sit in the refrigerator for one to three days before cooking—just don't forget that you already salted it!

DRIED BEANS: When cooking dried beans, you typically want to soak them in water prior to cooking. Adding a few teaspoons of salt per quart of water effectively reduces the cooking time because when heated, the saltwater breaks down the cells of the beans more quickly than plain water.

PASTA, POTATOES, AND RICE: Because starches do an excellent job of absorbing salt, salting the cooking water for these foods considerably enhances their flavor from the inside out. Use the guide of 1 to 2 tablespoons of kosher salt per 4 quarts (1 gallon) of water. Salt also makes pasta less sticky because it reduces

starch gelatinization, which is when heated water causes starchy foods such as pasta to swell.

VEGETABLES: When boiling or blanching vegetables, you want to salt the cooking water. This allows the salt to penetrate the vegetables, seasoning them from the inside out. Also, because plain water draws salts and other nutrients from vegetables, the addition of salt to the water reduces the amount of lost nutrients. Use the guideline of 1 to 2 tablespoons of kosher salt per 4 quarts (1 gallon) of water. When blanching vegetables, you can also season the iced blanching water, which will give the vegetables some additional flavor on the outer surface.

GUIDELINES FOR USING ACIDS

Another key method to seasoning food is to incorporate acids into your cooking. When using acids, I like to think about balance, because that is essentially what they do best: brighten the flavors of a dish through contrast and cause the seasonings to become cohesive. Acids in cooking include, but are not limited to, citrus juices, vinegars, wine, tomato, buttermilk, yogurt, sour cream, coffee, and cocoa powder. Many of us use acidic ingredients often without ever recognizing how they affect our cooking.

Here are some of the ways acids affect seasoning:

- Acids can minimize the need for salt in some instances because acidic compounds help us to recognize saltiness in foods. Studies have confirmed this phenomenon when using lemon juice and zest to flavor foods.
- Acids that are added to sweet foods not only add another dimension of flavor but also suppress some of that sweetness to make them more enjoyable.
- Acidic compounds are often added to marinades to help tenderize and enhance flavors. The acids cause the protein structure on the surface to weaken, which in turn softens the texture.
- Acids do an excellent job of contrasting or cut-

ting through the rich flavor of fat, which is why you often see a wedge of lemon offered with fried foods, or pickles served on a cheeseburger.

GUIDELINES FOR USING SPICES AND HERBS

Salt and acids aren't the only ways to get flavor into foods; there are also spices and herbs to consider. Herbs are the leafy green parts of a plant, and they can be fresh or dried. Spices are dried and typically come from roots, bark, berries, and seeds. As with salt and acids, herbs and spices are considered flavor enhancers, but they can also contribute to the color of a dish.

Here are some guidelines to follow for using herbs and spices:

- Fresh herbs are best added at the end of cooking, to finish a dish, keeping their flavor bright and vibrant. An example would be adding freshly chopped parsley at the end of braising Moroccan chicken tagine.

- Dried herbs need time to release their flavors, so they are best added during the cooking process. They are typically used when making braised dishes, stews, soups, and sauces. If you want to encourage the release of flavor, rub the dried herbs between your fingertips before adding them to the recipe. (Often you will use dried and fresh herbs in combination, but they will be added at different times during the cooking process.)

- When using spices, first make sure they are not expired! Ground spices don't last much longer than six months, whereas whole spices will last about four years. Buying whole spices and grinding them yourself will make a noticeable difference in their freshness and flavor. Spices are best stored in a cool, dry place.

- Heating spices—or even herbs for that matter—in hot oil helps to trigger chemical reactions that release flavor compounds. This technique, which is known as blooming, also distributes that flavor more efficiently throughout the entire dish.

SEASONING GLOSSARY

Understanding your ingredients is the first step to mastering seasoning. In this glossary, I've compiled a comprehensive list of essential salts, spices, and flavor enhancers you'll encounter throughout this book.

SALTS

DIAMOND CRYSTAL KOSHER SALT: A pure, flaky salt, known for its delicate texture and clean taste.

MALDON SEA SALT FLAKES: Pyramid-shaped salt crystals, with a briny flavor and crunchy texture.

SPICES

ALEPPO PEPPER FLAKES: Crushed dried chili with moderate heat balanced by fruity undertones.

DRIED BASIL: Dried basil leaf with warm, sweet, and minty undertones.

WHOLE BLACK PEPPERCORNS: Whole form of ground black pepper.

GROUND BLACK PEPPER: Finely crushed whole peppercorns that add warmth and pungency.

CHILI POWDER: A fragrant blend of spices offering earthy subtle heat.

DRIED CHIVES: Dried form of the fresh herb with a hint of onion flavor.

GROUND CINNAMON: Ground cinnamon bark with a sweet, woody aroma.

GROUND CLOVES: Powdered form of whole cloves with warm, spicy, and intense flavor.

GROUND CORIANDER: Ground seeds of the cilantro plant with citrusy, earthy nuttiness.

GROUND CUMIN: Ground seeds of the cumin plant, known for its earthy, slightly bitter, and aromatic taste.

DRIED DILL: Dried dill weed with a light and feathery texture, with sweet grassy notes.

MILD CURRY POWDER: A blend of warming spices, yielding a mildly spicy, aromatic, and complex flavor.

GARAM MASALA: An Indian spice blend with warming spices, known for its pungent, sweet, and spicy flavor.

GRANULATED GARLIC: Dehydrated garlic processed into granules with a concentrated garlic flavor.

GROUND GINGER: Dried ground ginger with a bold, spicy flavor.

MUSTARD POWDER: Ground mustard seeds with a notable spicy, tangy flavor.

GROUND NUTMEG: Grated nutmeg seed, known for its sweet, warm, and slightly nutty flavor.

ONION POWDER: Dried ground onion offering intense onion flavor.

DRIED OREGANO: Dried oregano leaves, recognized for their pungent, slightly bitter, and earthy undertones.

SWEET PAPRIKA: Dried ground sweet red peppers with a sweet, bitter, and slightly fruity flavor.

SMOKED PAPRIKA: Paprika with a rich, smoky flavor from smoking peppers over wood.

DRIED PARSLEY: Dried parsley leaves with a mild herbaceous flavor.

GROUND SAGE: Dried sage leaves ground into a powder, with piney, lemony notes.

SUMAC: Dried ground berries of wild sumac flowers with a tangy, lemony, and slightly fruity taste.

GROUND TURMERIC: Dried ground turmeric with a bitter, earthy flavor and a vibrant yellow-orange hue.

FLAVOR ENHANCERS

CHILI-GARLIC SAUCE: A spicy condiment made from chili peppers, garlic, and vinegar.

CHIPOTLE PEPPERS IN ADOBO: Smoked jalapeños canned in a tangy, spicy tomato-based sauce.

FISH SAUCE: A savory, umami-rich liquid made from fermented fish and salt.

HARISSA PASTE: A spicy and aromatic chili paste, made with dried red chilies, garlic, and various spices.

KIMCHI: Fermented Korean side dish made from vegetables, primarily Napa cabbage and radishes, with a blend of seasonings.

MATCHA POWDER: Finely ground powder of specially grown and processed green tea leaves.

MIRIN: A sweet, slightly syrupy rice wine used to add mild sweetness and depth.

POMEGRANATE MOLASSES: A tangy reduction of pomegranate juice, sweet and tart.

THAI GREEN CURRY PASTE: A fragrant, spicy paste commonly made with green chilies, lemongrass, galangal, and other Thai herbs and spices.

WHITE MISO: A fermented soybean paste with a light, slightly sweet flavor, for adding umami and depth.

CUP OZ

1 — 8

3/4 — 6

2/3

CUPS OZ

2 — 16

1 ml

1 — 1000

900

800

3/4 — 700

600

1/2 — 500

400

300

Microplane

ESSENTIAL TOOLS

Before diving in to the recipes, let's talk tools! One of the secrets to better home cooking is arming yourself with the right kitchen tools. Here's my go-to list of essentials that make cooking smoother and more enjoyable.

SMALL ESSENTIAL TOOLS

8-inch chef knife

Utility knife (or paring knife)

Serrated bread knife

Kitchen shears

Large cutting board

Small cutting board

Measuring cups (wet and dry)

Measuring spoons

Instant-read thermometer

Box grater

Fine mesh wire strainer

Stainless steel spider strainer

Stainless steel spatula

Silicone spatula

Wooden spoon

Balloon whisk

Pastry brush

Stainless steel tongs

Vegetable peeler

Citrus squeezer or rimmer

Bench scraper

Dough scraper

Pepper grinder

LARGE ESSENTIAL EQUIPMENT

Stand mixer with paddle, whisk, and dough hook attachments; or hand blender

12- or 14-cup food processor

Immersion blender or high-speed blender

Kitchen scale

Mixing bowls

Dutch oven

8- or 10-quart stockpot

10-inch nonstick sauté pan

4-quart saucepan

8- or 10-inch cast-iron skillet

9-by-13-inch glass baking dish

8½-by-5-inch loaf pan

8-by-8-inch baking dish

9-inch springform pan

Two rimmed half sheet pans

Wire rack

BEST STORING PRACTICES

Given my background as a trained chef, I'm always intrigued by how people arrange their refrigerators. While food storage safety is paramount in the culinary industry, I've often wondered why this vigilance doesn't always make its way to home kitchens. The position of food within your fridge significantly impacts its longevity. Most refrigerators contain both colder and warmer zones, with temperatures ranging between 33°F and 38°F. The coolest spots are often toward the back of the shelves, particularly near the fan and condenser, while the door shelves tend to be warmer.

I suggest an organization of items within your fridge that aligns foods with their temperature needs. This setup not only ensures optimal storage temperatures but also acts as a safeguard: The idea is that if any food from an upper shelf happens to drip, the items below won't be ruined. Thus, items that are typically cooked at a temperature high enough to kill any potential bacteria should be placed on lower shelves.

(OPTIMAL) REFRIGERATOR ORGANIZATION

Top Shelf

Ready-to-eat prepared foods

Leftovers in containers

Pickles and pickled products

Beverages

Middle Shelf

Eggs

Yogurt

Sour cream, cottage cheese, cream cheese

Tofu

Cold cuts and sliced cheese

Packaged shredded cheese

Bottom Shelf

Raw meat and poultry (placed on rimmed baking sheet or in plastic bin to contain any leakage)

Raw fish and shellfish (placed on rimmed baking sheet or in plastic bin to contain any leakage)

Vegetable and Fruit Crisper Drawers

Fresh vegetables

Herbs (rolled in damp paper towels and stored inside plastic bags)

Fresh fruit (if you don't have a fruit crisper drawer, store them on the top shelf)

Refrigerator Doors

Butter

Block cheeses

Condiments

Dressings and vinaigrettes

Beverages

NOTES ON THE FREEZER

- Refrain from obstructing the freezer's air vents with stacked items.
- Transfer meat from store packaging to flat, airtight zip-lock or vacuum-sealed bags, to avoid freezer burn.
- Store items such as nuts, seeds, and various flours in the freezer to extend their freshness.

CHAPTER 1

THE BASICS

Every home cook's journey begins with the basics—the foundational building blocks. By mastering these core recipes and techniques, you open the door to crafting countless other dishes.

Central to these foundations is understanding the basic art of seasoning. Salt, the world's most well-known seasoning, does more than just enhance food; it makes food taste like a better version of itself, working to balance flavors. Grasping the science behind it is often helpful—for instance, salt draws moisture from meat only for the meat to reabsorb a richer, salt-infused version of itself. This technique, known as dry brining, is used in Dry-Brined Pork Tenderloin (page 34), for example. The timing and nuances of salting will be a recurrent topic in this chapter and throughout the book.

Black pepper, on the other hand, is a spice, and doesn't just add heat—it's more about adding depth. That subtle heat that lingers on your tongue when you eat something sprinkled with pepper? That's the pepper working its magic, adding layers of complexity to your meals.

Shifting gears, let's consider the essential role of basic fats in everyday cooking. Extra virgin olive oil, known for its fruity, grassy, and peppery notes, is a culinary powerhouse. It does more than serve as a cooking oil, infusing dishes with a distinctive richness. It also shines as a finishing oil, imparting its unique flavor subtleties, such as in the Summer Tomato & Burrata Salad (page 26).

And butter? It's the epitome of richness. Beyond its role as a creamy, soft spread or a versatile ingredient, butter is crucial to the browning process, giving dishes that irresistible edge. When melted, and especially when browned, butter introduces flavorful nuances that are truly unparalleled, as in the Perfect Butter-Basted Rib Eye Steak (page 33). It's worth noting that whenever I mention butter in this book, I'm referring to American butter, available in both salted and unsalted varieties, with an 80 percent butterfat content.

Finally, everyday condiments, often overlooked in home kitchens, have the potential to be culinary game changers. For instance, ketchup and Worcestershire sauce are more than just condiments; they're flavor enhancers that infuse dishes with both taste and moisture, as demonstrated in the Juicy Turkey Burgers (page 29).

SAUTÉED MIXED VEGETABLES

The humble act of sautéing vegetables can transform them into a vibrant, delectable side dish. Success hinges on mastering the timing: Different vegetables, from the firm onion to the tender zucchini, require varied cooking times. A simple seasoning of garlic, salt, and pepper allows the natural flavors of the vegetables to shine through. The beauty of this recipe is its adaptability; feel free to switch up the veggies based on what's fresh and in season.

SERVES 4

PREP TIME: **10 minutes**
COOKING TIME: **10 minutes**
TOTAL TIME: **about 20 minutes**

2 to 3 tablespoons extra virgin olive oil

1 small yellow onion, halved and diced

1 medium red bell pepper, seeded, diced

1 medium zucchini or summer squash, diced

8 ounces white button mushrooms, sliced

2 garlic cloves, minced

1 to 2 teaspoons kosher salt

¼ teaspoon ground black pepper

1 Add the oil to a large stainless steel skillet over medium heat and add the onion, cooking until translucent, 3 to 4 minutes.

2 Add the red bell pepper and zucchini and cook for another 3 minutes, then add the mushrooms and cook for another 2 to 3 minutes before adding the garlic and cooking for another minute. Season with salt and pepper and allow to cool slightly before serving.

NOTE:

Feel free to substitute your favorite vegetables for the ones in this recipe, making sure to cook the harder vegetables such as onions or broccoli before the softer vegetables like mushrooms or peas.

FANCY ROASTED BABY CARROTS

These fancy baby carrots may look and taste as if they've been delicately crafted in a gourmet kitchen, but the process is as straightforward as it gets. Don't grab the bag labeled "baby carrots." Instead seek out true baby carrots, those that resemble miniature versions of their full-sized counterparts. Roasting at a high temperature accentuates the carrots' inherent sugars, creating a delightful caramelization. A honey drizzle over the warm carrots enhances their natural sweetness and creates a beautiful glaze. An effortlessly elegant side dish.

SERVES 4

PREP TIME: **5 minutes**
COOKING TIME: **35 minutes**
TOTAL TIME: **about 40 minutes**

1 pound baby carrots, peeled and tops removed

2 tablespoons extra virgin olive oil

1 teaspoon kosher salt

¼ teaspoon freshly cracked black pepper

2 teaspoons honey

1   Adjust your oven rack to the middle position and preheat the oven to 425°F. Line a rimmed baking sheet with parchment paper.

2   In a large mixing bowl, toss together the carrots, olive oil, salt, and pepper. Transfer to the parchment-lined baking sheet and spread out in an even layer.

3   Roast in the oven for 30 to 35 minutes, or until the carrots are tender and easily pierced with a fork. Remove from the oven and immediately drizzle with the honey, gently toss to coat, serve immediately.

SUMMER TOMATO & BURRATA SALAD

When my garden overflows with perfectly ripe heirloom tomatoes, there's one dish I never tire of and find myself returning to time and again, a true classic: tomato and burrata salad. This dish embodies the simplicity and delight of summer's bounty. Juicy, sun-ripened tomatoes combined with luxurious, soft burrata make for a delightful contrast in textures. A sprinkle of salt, crack of black pepper, and generous drizzle of olive oil are all it takes to make this salad one of the best things you will eat all summer.

SERVES 4 OR 5

TOTAL TIME: **10** minutes

One 8-ounce ball fresh burrata

2 to 3 ripe medium heirloom tomatoes, cut into wedges

1 cup ripe cherry tomatoes, halved

½ teaspoon kosher salt

¼ teaspoon freshly cracked black pepper

2 to 3 tablespoons extra virgin olive oil

1 tablespoon balsamic reduction (optional)

10 fresh basil leaves, roughly chopped

1   Place the burrata in the center of a large shallow serving bowl or rimmed plate. Artfully arrange the tomatoes around the burrata, then gently quarter the burrata. Season the tomatoes and burrata with salt and pepper.

2   Drizzle with olive oil and balsamic reduction, if desired, garnish with basil leaves, and serve immediately.

NOTE:

When they're in season, I enjoy adding ripe stone fruits like peaches, nectarines, and plums to my burrata salad. Feel free to mix it up and try different fruit combinations.

JUICY TURKEY BURGERS

Preparing the ideal turkey burger might seem like a challenge given the meat's lean profile, but the solution is easy. It's all about introducing flavor and moisture to the mix. Incorporating cooked onion, ketchup, and Worcestershire sauce ensures every bite is succulent. Offering homemade condiments is a pro move here, and I recommend either Roasted Garlic Aioli (page 45) or Special Burger Sauce (page 49) slathered generously on a toasted brioche burger bun.

SERVES 4

PREP TIME: **10 minutes**
COOKING TIME: **18 minutes**
TOTAL TIME: about **28 minutes**

1 tablespoon avocado or sunflower oil
½ small yellow onion, finely diced
1 tablespoon ketchup
1 teaspoon Worcestershire sauce
1 teaspoon granulated garlic
½ teaspoon kosher salt
¼ teaspoon ground black pepper
1 pound ground turkey
Cooking pan spray
4 brioche hamburger buns
Green lettuce leaves (optional)
Tomato slices (optional)
Pickles (optional)

1 Adjust the oven rack to the middle position and preheat to 350°F. Line a rimmed baking sheet with aluminum foil or parchment paper.

2 Add oil to a sauté pan over medium heat and cook the onions until just tender, 3 to 4 minutes. Remove from the heat and allow to cool slightly.

3 In a large mixing bowl, combine the cooked onion, ketchup, Worcestershire sauce, garlic, salt, pepper, and ground turkey. Shape the mixture into four equal-sized round patties, about 4 ounces each.

4 Spray a nonstick griddle or frying pan with cooking pan spray over medium-high heat, add the patties to the hot pan, in batches if needed, and cook for about 3 minutes per side or until a nice crust forms. Transfer the burgers to the prepared baking sheet and let them finish cooking in the oven until the center internal temperature reaches 160° to 165°F on an instant-read thermometer, 6 to 8 minutes.

5 Assemble the burgers onto the hamburger buns and, if desired, top with your favorite condiments and toppings, including lettuce, tomato slices, and pickles.

NOTES:

- You can grill these turkey burgers; just make sure to preheat the grill and oil the grates well.
- I recommend toasting your hamburger buns. To do this, spread about 1 teaspoon of mayonnaise or softened butter on each half of the buns. In batches, add the buns cut side down to a pan or griddle over medium heat, and cook for about 30 seconds or until toasted and golden brown.

SPATCHCOCK ROASTED CHICKEN

Few things embody comfort and versatility in the kitchen quite like a perfectly roasted chicken. Spatchcocking, or the art of removing the chicken's backbone, allows the bird to lie flat, ensuring more even cooking and a juicier result. The seasoning here is minimalistic: just salt, pepper, and butter. It's a combination that allows the chicken's natural savoriness to shine. While creamy mashed potatoes remain a classic pairing for roasted chicken, this dish also pairs beautifully with Za'atar Roasted Sweet Potato Wedges (page 175) and a crisp green salad.

SERVES 4 OR 5

PREP TIME: **15 minutes**
COOKING TIME: **45 minutes**
TOTAL TIME: **60 minutes**

One 4-pound whole chicken

1 tablespoon kosher salt, or more as needed

½ teaspoon ground black pepper

2 tablespoons avocado or sunflower oil

2 tablespoons salted butter, melted

1 Adjust the oven rack to the middle position and preheat the oven to 450°F.

2 To spatchcock the chicken: place it on a cutting board and use a sharp pair of kitchen shears to cut through the ribs and along either side of the chicken's backbone to remove it. Flatten the chicken by pressing firmly down on the breast bone, until you feel a pop.

3 Use paper towels to dry the chicken well. Liberally season the chicken all over the skin side and cavity side with salt and pepper. Then rub the oil over the chicken skin and transfer to a wire rack set inside an aluminum foil–lined rimmed baking sheet.

4 Roast the chicken for about 30 minutes. Then brush the melted butter all over the skin and cook for another 10 to 15 minutes or until the thickest part of the chicken breast reaches an internal temperature of 150° to 155°F on an instant-read thermometer.

5 Let the chicken rest for 5 to 10 minutes before carving and serving.

NOTE:

If the idea of spatchcocking a chicken at home is too intimidating, you can ask the butcher to do it for you. Prepackaged spatchcock chickens are also available nowadays.

PERFECT BUTTER-BASTED RIB EYE STEAK

The tender and incredibly flavorful rib eye is always my first choice when I crave a restaurant-quality steak at home. Picking the perfect steak is an art: It's about opting for one with intricate fat marbling, a relatively small "eye" (the center muscle), and a generous cap muscle, which is the steak's best part. While many home cooks overlook the step of butter basting, it's a game changer. This technique enhances the steak's overall browning and infuses a deep, nutty, rich flavor.

SERVES 1 OR 2

PREP TIME: **5 minutes**
COOKING TIME: **10 minutes**
TOTAL TIME: **15 minutes, plus rest time**

One 14- to 16-ounce boneless rib eye steak, 1 to 1½ inches thick

1 to 2 teaspoons kosher salt

½ teaspoon freshly cracked black pepper

2 tablespoons avocado or sunflower oil

1 tablespoon salted butter

1   Pat the steak dry with a paper towel and allow to sit at room temperature for 25 to 30 minutes. Immediately before cooking, season both sides liberally with salt and pepper.

2   Add the oil to a 10-inch cast-iron pan or stainless steel skillet over high heat until the oil starts to smoke. Add the steak to the pan and sear, flipping the steak every minute or so for 6 to 8 minutes, searing the edges as well, until the steak is well browned and the internal temperature reaches 120°F on an instant-read thermometer. Reduce the heat to medium, add the butter to the pan, tilt the pan to one side, and use a large spoon to continuously baste the foamy butter over the top of the steak, cooking for another 1 to 2 minutes, until the steak reaches an internal temperature of 130° to 135°F for medium-rare.

3   Transfer the steak to a cutting board and allow to rest for at least 5 minutes before slicing and serving.

NOTE:

You can substitute New York strip steak, T-bone steak, or porterhouse steak for the rib eye.

DRY-BRINED PORK TENDERLOIN

Dry brining is essentially a process of salting meat before cooking. This technique allows the salt to deeply penetrate the muscle, promising well-seasoned, juicy meat. Keep the seasoning simple: A blend of salt and pepper allows the pork's naturally sweet, mild flavor to shine. This recipe serves as a starting point: introduce dried herbs, granulated garlic, or onion powder for added depth. Thinly slice the tenderloin and serve atop Arugula, Fig & Walnut Salad with Maple Balsamic Vinaigrette (page 63) for an elegant, light meal.

SERVES 3 OR 4

PREP TIME: **5 minutes**
DRY BRINE TIME: **8+ hours**
COOKING TIME: **28 minutes**
TOTAL TIME: **8 hours 33 minutes**

One 1¼-pound pork tenderloin
1 to 2 teaspoons kosher salt
½ teaspoon ground black pepper
2 tablespoons avocado or sunflower oil

1 Pat dry the pork tenderloin with paper towels. Season the pork all over with salt and pepper and transfer to a wire rack set inside a rimmed baking sheet. Refrigerate the pork for at least 8 hours or up to 24 hours.

2 Adjust the oven rack to the center position and preheat to 425°F.

3 Add the oil to a cast-iron pan or a stainless steel skillet over medium-high heat until the oil begins to shimmer. Sear the pork on all sides, 2 to 3 minutes per side.

4 Transfer the pork to the oven for 15 to 20 minutes, or until the center reaches an internal temperature of 140°F on an instant-read thermometer.

5 Let the pork rest for at least 10 minutes before slicing and serving.

NOTE:

You may need to halve the pork tenderloin to fit it in the cast-iron pan or stainless steel skillet. Make sure to check the internal temperature in the thickest part of the meat for doneness.

RESTAURANT-STYLE SEARED SALMON

To achieve that restaurant-quality, golden brown sear on your salmon, all you need is a really hot cast-iron or stainless steel skillet, the right amount of oil, and a touch of salt and pepper. While the focus here is on skinless fillets, I've included a cooking note for any skin-on enthusiasts. This salmon makes a stellar protein boost to any salad. Consider trying it atop the Banh Mi Salad with Nuoc Cham Vinaigrette (page 64), or serve it alongside the Fried Brussels Sprouts with Caper Vinaigrette (page 67).

SERVES 2

PREP TIME: **5 minutes**
COOKING TIME: **8 minutes**
TOTAL TIME: **about 13 minutes**

Two 6-ounce salmon fillets, skinned
1 teaspoon kosher salt
¼ teaspoon freshly cracked black pepper
2 tablespoons avocado or sunflower oil

1 Let the salmon sit at room temperature for 10 to 15 minutes. Pat the salmon dry with paper towels. Immediately before cooking, season the salmon on both sides with salt and pepper.

2 Add the oil to a cast-iron pan or stainless steel skillet over medium-high heat, until the oil starts shimmering. Reduce the heat to medium and carefully place the salmon flesh side down in the pan and cook for 3 to 4 minutes, or until nicely browned on that side. Turn the salmon over with a spatula or tongs and cook for another 3 minutes, or until the center reaches an internal temperature of 130° to 135°F on an instant-read thermometer. Serve immediately.

NOTE:

If cooking salmon with the skin on, place the salmon in the pan skin side down. Press down gently on the fillets for about 10 seconds to make sure the skin makes contact with the pan (or it will curl) and cook for about 4 minutes, before turning and cooking for another 2 to 3 minutes.

CONDIMENTS & DIPPING SAUCES

Among the myriad culinary debates, one topic that often sparks contentious discussions is that of condiments, sauces, and dips. Delving in to this subject can quickly lead down a rabbit hole of strong opinions about distinctions and information overload. To simplify matters, I'm going to focus on the difference between condiments and dipping sauces, leaving the realm of true sauces for another chapter (page 123).

I like to think of a condiment as a versatile companion to food. It can add specific flavors, enhance existing ones, or even alter the texture of a dish. Unlike essential ingredients, condiments are often added after the cooking process is finished, and they have the power to take a dish from good to great. For instance, Classic Mayonnaise (page 42) serves as an amazing base for creating a wide range of other condiments, such as our Special Burger Sauce (page 49).

On the other hand, a dip, which could be considered a condiment, is a thick and often creamy sauce that is used to dip food into. Typically made with a combination of a fat, acid, and flavorings such as herbs and spices, dips complement and enhance the flavors of various foods while adding delightful textures. For example, our Blue Cheese Dip (page 48), known for its addictive salty and funky flavor, not only adds a delightful taste to dishes but also helps to tone down spicy flavors.

While it may be convenient to grab condiments and dipping sauces from the supermarket shelves, it's worth considering the advantages of making them at home. Store-bought options often contain excessive amounts of sugar and chemical preservatives to prolong their shelf life. In contrast, homemade condiments and dipping sauces not only offer superior flavor but also grant you the freedom to personalize the taste according to your preferences. The recipes included in this chapter are designed to be accessible, and many have relatively short ingredient lists.

CLASSIC MAYONNAISE

Mastering homemade mayonnaise requires just five minutes and serves as the base for an array of condiments, dips, sauces, and dishes.

MAKES ABOUT 1 CUP

TOTAL TIME: **5 minutes**

1 large egg, room temperature
1 tablespoon fresh lemon juice
1 teaspoon white wine vinegar
1 teaspoon Dijon mustard
½ to 1 teaspoon kosher salt
1 cup avocado or sunflower neutral oil

1   Add the egg, lemon juice, vinegar, Dijon mustard, and salt to a large measuring cup or plastic quart container that will fit the head of an immersion blender. It's important that the egg mixture reaches the blades of your immersion blender to allow the emulsion to work.

2   Pour the oil on top and allow it to settle for a minute. Place the immersion blender in the cup or container and press it firmly to the bottom. Turn to high speed while continuing to press against the bottom. You will notice the mayonnaise starting to form and emulsify. Slowly move the immersion blender up and down until fully combined.

3   Stir the mayonnaise and taste for seasoning before storing it in an airtight container and placing it in the refrigerator for up to 2 weeks.

NOTES:

- Make sure the mouth of the glass measuring cup or container fits the width of the immersion blender. I suggest using a 4-cup OXO Good Grips silicone measuring cup or a plastic quart container.

- If your mayonnaise is watery, it has not emulsified correctly. You can let the mixture settle and then try blending it again, pressing the immersion blender firmly to the bottom of the cup or container.

- If you are concerned about using raw egg in this recipe, use a store-bought pasteurized egg.

Classic Mayonnaise

Bravas Sauce

Blue Cheese Dip

Roasted Garlic Aioli

Tartar Sauce

Sweet Basil Aioli

SWEET BASIL AIOLI

Infusing aromatic sweet fresh basil and pungent garlic into creamy mayonnaise results in this delightful aioli, adding a fresh burst of flavor to whatever you pair it with.

MAKES ABOUT 1 CUP

TOTAL TIME: **3 minutes**

1 cup Classic Mayonnaise (page 42) or store-bought

½ cup fresh basil leaves, finely chopped

1 small garlic clove, minced

1 teaspoon fresh lemon juice

½ teaspoon granulated garlic

In a small mixing bowl, whisk together all the ingredients until well combined. Taste for seasoning. This aioli will last for up to 2 weeks stored in an airtight container in the refrigerator.

ROASTED GARLIC AIOLI

Roasting garlic transforms its natural sharpness into a mellow, sweet, and nutty flavor. When blended into mayonnaise, the result is a lusciously rich aioli, perfect for spreading on a burger or sandwich, or for dipping fries.

MAKES ABOUT 1 CUP

TOTAL TIME: about 50 minutes

1 garlic bulb
1 to 2 teaspoons extra virgin olive oil
1 cup Classic Mayonnaise (page 42)
   or store-bought
1 teaspoon fresh lemon juice
¼ teaspoon black pepper

1   Preheat the oven to 400°F.

2   Peel off most of the loose, papery outer layers around the garlic bulb, while leaving the head intact. Slice off the top of the garlic bulb, exposing the tops of the cloves. Place the garlic bulb on top of a piece of aluminum foil, then drizzle with the olive oil and wrap tightly.

3   Roast in the oven for 40 to 50 minutes, depending on the size of the garlic bulb. Start testing it after about 40 minutes. When done, the center clove should be completely soft and easy to pierce with a toothpick or knife. Remove the garlic bulb from the oven and allow it to cool. Once cool, press or squeeze the bottom of the garlic bulb to push the cloves out of the paper. Chop up the roasted garlic cloves and add them to a small mixing bowl.

4   Add the rest of the ingredients to the mixing bowl and whisk everything together until well combined. Taste and adjust the seasoning as you like. This aioli will last for up to 2 weeks stored in an airtight container in the refrigerator.

TARTAR SAUCE

Homemade tartar sauce is definitely worth the effort, as it's much better than anything you can buy at the store. This is a punchy sauce, largely due to the cornichon pickles, and it is exactly what I crave with most seafood dishes.

MAKES ABOUT 1½ CUPS

TOTAL TIME: **8 minutes**

1 cup Classic Mayonnaise (page 42) or store-bought

½ teaspoon fresh lemon zest

1 tablespoon fresh lemon juice

1 garlic clove, minced

¼ teaspoon ground black pepper

½ cup cornichon pickles, finely diced

1 tablespoon fresh dill, finely chopped

2 teaspoons fresh parsley, finely chopped

1   In a small mixing bowl, whisk together all the ingredients, except for the cornichon, dill, and parsley, until smooth.

2   Add the cornichon, dill, and parsley to the mixture and stir until well combined. Taste for seasoning. This sauce will last for up to a week stored in an airtight container in the refrigerator.

NOTE:

You can substitute dill pickles for the cornichon pickles.

BRAVAS SAUCE

Our version of traditional bravas sauce has quickly become a Feast & Fettle favorite! We've taken the classic blend of olive oil, smoked paprika, tomato, and vinegar and elevated it with rich mayonnaise, resulting in a flavor profile that's both creamy and smoky. While we typically serve this with roasted potatoes, honestly, it's good on everything.

MAKES ABOUT 1 CUP

TOTAL TIME: 8 minutes

1 tablespoon extra virgin olive oil

1 medium shallot, diced

1 garlic clove, minced or grated

2 teaspoons smoked paprika

½ teaspoon kosher salt, plus more to taste

2 teaspoons tomato paste

¾ cup Classic Mayonnaise (page 42) or store-bought

1 teaspoon white wine vinegar

1 tablespoon water

½ teaspoon hot sauce, or more to taste

1   Add the olive oil to a sauté pan over medium heat. Add the shallot and cook for about 2 minutes before adding the garlic and cooking for another minute. Add the smoked paprika, salt, and tomato paste to the shallot mixture to cook for another minute before turning off the heat and setting aside to cool a bit.

2   To a large glass measuring cup or quart container, add the mayonnaise, onion mixture, vinegar, water, and hot sauce. Using an immersion blender or high-speed blender, blend until smooth. Taste for seasoning. This sauce will last for up to a week stored in an airtight container in the refrigerator.

BLUE CHEESE DIP

This dip highlights the bold, creamy, and funky flavor of blue cheese, as it melds seamlessly with mayonnaise and sour cream. While it's the perfect pairing for chicken wings or crudités, a splash of milk transforms it into the ideal blue cheese dressing.

MAKES ABOUT 1 CUP

TOTAL TIME: **5 minutes**

½ cup **Classic Mayonnaise (page 42) or store-bought**
½ cup **sour cream**
1 tablespoon **buttermilk**
½ teaspoon **Worcestershire sauce**
1 **small garlic clove, minced**
¼ teaspoon **black pepper**
¼ cup **crumbled blue cheese**

In a small mixing bowl, whisk together all the ingredients except for the blue cheese until smooth. Then stir in the blue cheese, breaking it up a bit, until well combined. Taste for seasoning. This dip will last for up to a week stored in an airtight container in the refrigerator.

SPECIAL BURGER SAUCE

This secret sauce (pun intended) is what every burger—and chicken tender—has been waiting for! Crafted from a blend of choice condiments, its sweet and tangy taste is truly addictive.

MAKES ABOUT 1 CUP

TOTAL TIME: **5 minutes**

¾ **cup Classic Mayonnaise (page 42) or store-bought**

1½ **tablespoons sweet relish**

1 **tablespoon ketchup**

1 **tablespoon yellow mustard**

1½ **teaspoons apple cider vinegar**

1 **teaspoon paprika**

½ **teaspoon granulated garlic**

½ **teaspoon onion powder**

In a small mixing bowl, whisk together all the ingredients until well combined. Taste for seasoning. This sauce will last for up to a week stored in an airtight container in the refrigerator.

Cucumber
Raita

Whipped
Feta Dip

Tzatziki
Sauce

Avocado
Lime Crema

AVOCADO LIME CREMA

When I'm craving something a bit more flavorful than plain sour cream, this is my go-to. Creamy avocado mixed with sour cream and mayo, seasoned with fresh lime juice and a touch of honey, creates a perfectly balanced crema. It's great dolloped on tacos, fajitas, and so much more.

MAKES ABOUT 2 CUPS

TOTAL TIME: **5 minutes**

1 cup sour cream

¼ cup Classic Mayonnaise (page 42) or store-bought

1 ripe avocado, halved and pitted

2 teaspoons fresh lime juice

½ teaspoon honey

½ teaspoon kosher salt

2 tablespoons avocado or sunflower oil

Add all the ingredients except the oil to the bowl of a food processor fitted with the S blade. Run the food processor while slowly pouring in the oil, until the mixture is well blended. This will take 30 seconds to 1 minute. Taste for seasoning. This crema will last for up to 3 days stored in an airtight container in the refrigerator.

CUCUMBER RAITA

This creamy, crunchy, spiced Indian condiment combines cooling cucumber with tart yogurt and fresh herbs. Typically served alongside rice, meat, and curry dishes, it's the ideal complement to counteract the heat of spicy dishes.

MAKES ABOUT 1 CUP

TOTAL TIME: **8 minutes**

1 cup whole-milk Greek yogurt

½ teaspoon ground cumin

¼ teaspoon garam masala (optional)

½ teaspoon kosher salt

½ cup seedless cucumber, diced small

1 tablespoon finely chopped fresh cilantro

1 tablespoon finely chopped fresh mint

In a small mixing bowl, whisk together all the ingredients except for the cucumber, cilantro, and mint until smooth. Then add the cucumber, cilantro, and mint, stirring until well combined. Taste for seasoning. This raita will last for up to a week stored in an airtight container in the refrigerator.

TZATZIKI SAUCE

A staple in Mediterranean and Greek kitchens, this refreshing sauce combines grated cucumber, tangy yogurt, fresh garlic, and herbs. There are countless ways to enjoy it, but my favorites include serving alongside grilled meats and vegetables, stirring into grain salads, or spreading on a piece of fresh pita bread.

MAKES ABOUT 2 CUPS

TOTAL TIME: 8 minutes

¾ cup whole-milk Greek yogurt

⅓ cup Classic Mayonnaise (page 42) or store-bought

3 teaspoons extra virgin olive oil

1 teaspoon fresh lemon juice

1 garlic clove, minced

½ teaspoon ground cumin

½ teaspoon kosher salt

1 cup seedless cucumber, grated and drained

2 teaspoons finely chopped fresh dill

1 teaspoon finely chopped fresh parsley

In a small mixing bowl, whisk together all the ingredients except for the cucumber, dill, and parsley until smooth. Then add the cucumber, dill, and parsley, stirring until well combined. Taste for seasoning. This sauce will last for up to a week stored in an airtight container in the refrigerator.

WHIPPED FETA DIP

Whipping together salty feta with thick Greek yogurt and olive oil makes for an irresistibly smooth and tangy dip. Use it as a spread for lamb or veggie burgers, or as a dip with raw or roasted vegetables and pita chips.

MAKES ABOUT 2 CUPS

TOTAL TIME: **5 minutes**

One 8-ounce block feta cheese, crumbled

1 cup whole-milk Greek yogurt

1 tablespoon extra virgin olive oil, plus more to drizzle

1 garlic clove, minced

½ teaspoon dried oregano

¼ teaspoon Aleppo pepper flakes

1   Add the feta cheese, Greek yogurt, olive oil, and garlic to the bowl of a food processor fitted with the S blade and process until smooth. Taste for seasoning.

2   Scoop the feta mixture into a serving bowl and sprinkle the dried oregano and Aleppo pepper over the top. Drizzle with a bit more olive oil over the top and serve. This dip will last for up to a week stored in an airtight container in the refrigerator.

NOTES:

- You can substitute crushed red pepper flakes for the Aleppo pepper; just keep in mind that they are spicier.

- If making ahead, scoop the whipped feta into an airtight storage container and sprinkle the dried oregano and Aleppo pepper over the top before covering with the lid.

SWEET SUMMER TOMATO JAM

Vine-ripened tomatoes simmered low and slow with brown sugar, a splash of lemon juice, and a pinch of nutmeg produce a luscious sauce with a jammy consistency. It's an ideal ketchup alternative that gives ordinary dishes an elevated twist.

MAKES ABOUT 2 CUPS

TOTAL TIME: about 90 minutes

1 pound vine-ripened tomatoes, cored and roughly chopped
½ cup brown sugar
¼ cup water
2 tablespoons fresh lemon juice
½ teaspoon kosher salt
¼ teaspoon ground nutmeg
¼ teaspoon freshly cracked black pepper

1 Combine all the ingredients in a heavy-bottomed medium saucepan.

2 Bring the mixture to a boil over medium-high heat, then reduce the heat to low and simmer, stirring occasionally until the mixture has a thick jam-like consistency and can coat the back of a wooden spoon. This should take 60 to 90 minutes. Adjust the seasoning to taste, remove the saucepan from the heat, and allow the mixture to cool to room temperature. Transfer the tomato jam into an airtight container and store in the refrigerator for up to 2 weeks.

NOTE:

If tomatoes are out of season, substitute with store-bought ripe plum or Roma tomatoes.

PEACH BBQ SAUCE

Taking BBQ sauce to the next level, this recipe melds classic condiments like ketchup, Worcestershire, and Dijon with the sweetness of peaches, brown sugar, and molasses. The addition of fresh rosemary brings a depth of flavor that truly sets it apart.

MAKES ABOUT 2 CUPS

TOTAL TIME: about 30 minutes

½ cup ketchup

¼ cup light brown sugar

4 ounces frozen peaches

2 tablespoons molasses

2 tablespoons apple cider vinegar

1 tablespoon Worcestershire sauce

1 tablespoon Dijon mustard

1 tablespoon fresh rosemary, finely chopped

½ teaspoon granulated garlic

½ teaspoon onion powder

½ teaspoon black pepper

1 Combine all the ingredients in a heavy-bottomed medium saucepan.

2 Bring the mixture to a boil over medium-high heat, then reduce heat to low and simmer, stirring occasionally for about 30 minutes, or until the mixture has thick consistency and can coat the back of a wooden spoon.

3 Using an immersion blender or a high-speed blender, blend until smooth. Taste for seasoning and cool. Transfer the sauce into an airtight container and store in the refrigerator for up to 2 weeks.

HONEY-DIJON DIPPING SAUCE

This isn't your typical honey-mustard sauce. With its pronounced tang from the blend of Dijon and yellow mustard, the honey's sweetness balances out the sharper notes. Perfect for dipping chicken tenders, soft pretzels, or adding a burst of flavor to wraps and sandwiches.

MAKES ABOUT 1 CUP

TOTAL TIME: **5 minutes**

½ **cup honey**

3 tablespoons Dijon mustard

2 tablespoons yellow mustard

2 tablespoons avocado or sunflower oil, or other neutral oil

2 tablespoons apple cider vinegar

1 teaspoon kosher salt

In a small mixing bowl, whisk together all the ingredients until well combined. Taste for seasoning. This sauce will last for up to 2 weeks stored in an airtight container in the refrigerator.

NOTE:

If you want to make a more traditional creamy honey-mustard sauce, add 1 to 2 tablespoons of mayonnaise to the recipe.

CHAPTER 3

DRESSINGS & VINAIGRETTES

At Feast & Fettle, we love creating tempting, mouthwatering, and inventive salad offerings. In fact, our seasonally inspired, artfully created salads played a pivotal role in setting us apart from other meal delivery services from the get-go.

A few foundational principles we adhere to at Feast & Fettle when constructing great salads are:

- *Start with a flavorful and fresh base.* Remember, it doesn't always have to be green lettuce! For example, you can use shredded cabbage or shaved Brussels sprouts.
- *Each component of the salad should contribute its own unique element,* either in terms of flavor or texture. For instance, pair sweet elements with salty counterparts, or rich components with something acidic, such as dried figs and shaved Parmesan, or pickled red onion and goat cheese.
- *A crunch factor is key to most great salads.* Consider adding homemade croutons, toasted nuts and seeds, or even chips or crackers.
- *Always dress the base of the salad before serving to ensure an even distribution of dressing or vinaigrette.* Your hands are actually the best tool for this, but if you prefer tongs, remember to be gentle. Afterward, transfer the dressed base to a serving dish and then add your additional components or toppings.

The secret behind our standout salads lies in the accompanying house-made dressings and vinaigrettes. My goal here is to show you the benefits of creating these at home, rather than reaching for store-bought alternatives.

Dressings or vinaigrettes are essentially sauces that enhance salads and prepared or chilled vegetables and fruits. The key distinction is that dressings typically have a creamy consistency, thanks to ingredients like mayonnaise, sour cream, or buttermilk; while vinaigrettes are a blend of an acidic component (like vinegar or lemon juice) and oil.

Dressings and vinaigrettes have applications beyond just green salads. Consider using them in dishes like Fried Brussels Sprouts with Caper Vinaigrette (page 67) or Greek Quinoa Salad with Creamy Greek Dressing (page 72).

ARUGULA, FIG & WALNUT SALAD

with Maple Balsamic Vinaigrette

Born from a client request during my time as a private chef, this salad quickly became a Feast & Fettle favorite. It's the ideal winter salad, brimming with robust flavors and textures. The only fresh produce you'll need is arugula. The vinaigrette, a harmonious blend of tangy and sweet, complements the peppery arugula, the sharp saltiness of the shaved Parmesan, and the concentrated sweetness of the dried figs. Toasting the walnuts not only reduces their inherent bitterness but also introduces a satisfying crunch, adding another dimension to this deceptively simple salad.

SERVES 4

PREP TIME: **10 minutes**
COOKING TIME: **10 minutes**
TOTAL TIME: **about 20 minutes**

FOR THE VINAIGRETTE
½ **cup avocado or sunflower oil**
⅓ **cup balsamic vinegar**
3 **tablespoons maple syrup**
2 **teaspoons Dijon mustard**
¼ **teaspoon kosher salt**

FOR THE SALAD
½ **cup raw walnuts, halved**
8 **ounces (6 to 7 cups) baby arugula**
8 **dried Mission figs, sliced**
½ **small red onion, thinly sliced**
½ **cup shaved Parmesan cheese**

1 To prepare the vinaigrette: Add all the ingredients to a high-speed blender and blend until emulsified. Taste for seasoning. Set aside. This vinaigrette will last up to 2 weeks stored in an airtight container in the refrigerator.

2 To prepare the salad: Preheat the oven to 325°F. Spread the walnuts on a rimmed baking sheet and roast for 10 minutes, or until lightly browned and fragrant. Remove the walnuts from the oven and allow them to cool. Once cool, roughly chop and set aside.

3 Add the arugula to a medium mixing bowl with ¼ to ½ cup of vinaigrette and toss to combine. Transfer the arugula to a large serving bowl and top with the toasted walnuts, figs, onion, and Parmesan. Serve immediately.

NOTE:

When fresh figs are in season, feel free to swap out the dried figs for fresh.

BANH MI SALAD
with Nuoc Cham Vinaigrette

The appeal of a traditional banh mi sandwich lies in the interplay of flavors and textures. You get crispy bread, tangy pickled carrot and daikon, a crunch from the cucumber, and a fresh herbal burst from the cilantro. This salad is a deconstructed version of the sandwich, embracing all the components you know and love, and making it a bit more approachable. The star of the dish—the pickled carrot and daikon—are essentially refrigerator pickles. They are remarkably easy to prepare. Simply immerse your prepped veggies in a vinegar solution, pop them in the fridge, and in a few hours you'll have flavor-packed pickles ready at your convenience!

SERVES 4

PREP TIME: **15 minutes**
MARINATING TIME: **2-plus hours**
COOKING TIME: **20 minutes**
TOTAL TIME: **2 hours 35 minutes**

FOR THE VINAIGRETTE
¼ cup fresh lime juice
¼ cup avocado or sunflower oil
3 tablespoons granulated sugar
2 tablespoons water
1 tablespoon fish sauce
1 teaspoon chili-garlic sauce
½ red Thai chili, thinly sliced

FOR THE PICKLES
2 medium carrots, peeled, julienned
1 medium daikon radish, peeled, julienned
½ cup seasoned rice vinegar
1 cup water
¼ cup granulated sugar
1 teaspoon kosher salt

FOR THE SALAD
1 French or Vietnamese baguette
¼ cup avocado or sunflower oil
½ teaspoon kosher salt
2 to 3 romaine lettuce hearts, washed and chopped
1 cup fresh cilantro leaves
½ English cucumber, thinly sliced
¼ cup roasted salted peanuts, chopped

1 To make the vinaigrette: Combine all the ingredients except for the Thai chili in a high-speed blender and blend until combined. Add the Thai chili and pulse a few times. Taste for seasoning and set aside. This vinaigrette will last for up to 2 weeks stored in an airtight container in the refrigerator.

2 To make the pickles: Add the carrots and daikon to a clean mason jar or glass mixing bowl.

3 Combine the vinegar, water, sugar, and salt in a small saucepan and bring to a boil. Once boiling, take off the heat and pour over the vegetables. Let cool to room temperature, then cover and refrigerate for at least 2 hours and up to 3 weeks.

4 To prepare the salad: Heat the oven to 375°F. Line a rimmed baking sheet with parchment paper.

5 Slice the bread in half and cut into ½- to 1-inch cubes. Toss the bread, oil, and salt in a large mixing bowl. Transfer the seasoned bread to the baking sheet and bake for 15 to 20 minutes, tossing halfway through, or until golden brown. Set aside to cool completely.

6 Add the lettuce, cilantro leaves, cucumber, half of the pickled carrot and daikon, and 1 cup of croutons to a large mixing bowl. Pour half of the vinaigrette over the top and toss to combine. Transfer the dressed salad to a large serving bowl and garnish with the chopped peanuts; add more vinaigrette if needed. Serve immediately.

FRIED BRUSSELS SPROUTS
with Caper Vinaigrette

Have you ever eaten those amazingly crispy Brussels sprouts at a restaurant and wondered how to achieve that level of deliciousness at home? The secret—deep frying! By fully enveloping the sprouts in hot oil, you quickly achieve that deep caramelization and irresistible crunch. While a sprinkle of kosher salt is all you really need to complete the dish, try taking it a step further with a tangy caper vinaigrette drizzled over the top. The bright acidity from the capers and lemon juice gives a refreshing finish to these deeply savory sprouts.

SERVES 4

PREP TIME: **15 minutes**
COOKING TIME: **10 minutes**
TOTAL TIME: about **25 minutes**

FOR THE VINAIGRETTE
¼ cup avocado or sunflower oil
¼ cup capers, drained and chopped
2 tablespoons lemon juice
1 tablespoon honey
1 garlic clove, grated
¼ teaspoon red chili flakes
¼ teaspoon kosher salt

FOR THE BRUSSELS SPROUTS
2 cups avocado or sunflower oil
1 pound Brussels sprouts, trimmed and halved lengthwise
½ teaspoon kosher salt

1   To prepare the vinaigrette: Add all the ingredients to a bowl and whisk vigorously to combine. Set aside. If the mixture separates, whisk again before serving. This vinaigrette will last for up to 2 weeks stored in an airtight container in the refrigerator.

2   Next, prepare the Brussels sprouts. In a pot with high sides, such as a Dutch oven or wok, heat the oil over medium-high heat until the temperature reaches about 350°F.

3   Meanwhile, set up a paper towel–lined rimmed baking sheet fitted with a wire rack.

4   Pat the Brussels sprouts dry with paper towels. Carefully add half of them to the hot oil, frying and turning frequently until they turn deeply golden brown and crisp, about 5 minutes. Use a slotted spoon or spider strainer to transfer the fried sprouts to the wire rack, immediately seasoning with salt. Repeat with the remaining sprouts.

5   Add the fried sprouts to a mixing bowl and spoon the vinaigrette over the top—you may not need to use the entire amount. Toss to evenly coat. Transfer to a serving bowl or plate and serve immediately.

NOTE:

Due to their high moisture content, Brussels sprouts can cause oil to sputter when fried. Using a fine mesh splatter screen will help prevent an oily stovetop mess.

APPLE & SHAVED FENNEL SALAD

with Apple Cider Vinaigrette

Every fall when the leaves start changing, we bring this salad back into regular rotation on the Feast & Fettle menu. The apple cider vinaigrette brilliantly ties together the crisp green apple, the subtle hint of anise from the fennel, and the tangy sweetness of the dried cranberries. What I love about this salad is its versatility—its acidic elements do a remarkable job of balancing out a heavy meal, providing a fresh, flavorful contrast.

SERVES 4

PREP TIME: **10 minutes**
COOKING TIME: **8 minutes**
TOTAL TIME: **about 18 minutes**

FOR THE VINAIGRETTE
½ cup avocado or sunflower oil
¼ cup apple cider vinegar
2 tablespoons fresh lemon juice
2 tablespoons honey
1 tablespoon Dijon mustard
1 garlic clove, smashed
½ teaspoon kosher salt

FOR THE SALAD
¼ cup sliced almonds
8 ounces (6 to 7 cups) baby green leaf lettuce
1 small fennel bulb, stalks and fronds removed, thinly sliced
1 Granny Smith apple, cored and sliced
¼ cup dried cranberries
¼ cup crumbled goat cheese

1   Begin by preparing the vinaigrette. Add all the ingredients to a high-speed blender and blend until emulsified. Taste for seasoning and set aside. This vinaigrette will last for up to 2 weeks stored in an airtight container in the refrigerator.

2   To prepare the salad: Preheat the oven to 325°F. Spread the almonds on a rimmed baking sheet. Roast for 8 minutes, or until lightly browned and fragrant.

3   Add the lettuce, fennel, and apples to a large mixing bowl with about half of the vinaigrette and toss to combine. Transfer to a large serving bowl and top with the dried cranberries, goat cheese, and toasted almonds. Serve immediately.

NOTES:

- To keep the apple from turning brown as you prepare the salad, submerge the apple slices in a saltwater solution made with 1 cup warm water and ½ teaspoon kosher salt for 5 to 10 minutes, and then drain.

- This salad would be delicious with blue cheese, Gorgonzola, or Cheddar substituted for the goat cheese.

NAPA CABBAGE SLAW

with Sweet Sesame Dressing

Napa cabbage, also known as Chinese cabbage, has a slightly sweeter flavor and more tender texture compared to basic green or red cabbage. These qualities make it an ideal candidate for a slaw-style salad. In this recipe, the addition of shredded carrots, snow peas, and scallions add brilliant pops of color and delightful crunch. Tying everything together is an addictive dressing, which boasts a creamy texture and a toasted sesame flavor profile that strikes a perfect balance between sweet and subtly acidic. This slaw makes for a refreshing side dish, and, if you want to turn it into a meal, just add your protein of choice for an easy, delicious entrée.

SERVES 4

TOTAL TIME: **15 minutes**

FOR THE DRESSING
½ cup **Classic Mayonnaise (page 42)** or store-bought
⅓ cup **rice vinegar**
3 tablespoons **granulated sugar**
2 teaspoons **sesame oil**
1 teaspoon **Dijon mustard**
1 teaspoon **toasted sesame seeds**
½ teaspoon **kosher salt**

FOR THE SALAD
1 medium head **Napa cabbage,** shredded
1 cup **shredded carrot**
4 ounces (about 1 cup) **snow peas,** thinly sliced on the bias
½ cup **thinly sliced scallions**
2 teaspoons **toasted sesame seeds**

1 To prepare the dressing: Add all the ingredients to a high-speed blender and blend until emulsified. Taste for seasoning and set aside. This dressing will last for up to a week stored in an airtight container in the refrigerator.

2 To assemble the slaw: Add all the ingredients except for the sesame seeds to a large mixing bowl. Pour half of the dressing over the top and toss to combine. Transfer the slaw to a large serving bowl and garnish with the sesame seeds; add more dressing if needed. Serve immediately.

GREEK QUINOA SALAD
with Creamy Greek Dressing

Hearty quinoa and chickpeas are infused with a creamy, tangy, herb-infused dressing and then tossed with crunchy cucumbers and a burst of sweet cherry tomatoes for a salad that is as flavorful as it is filling. The addition of crumbled feta and kalamata olives adds a delightful briny pop to the dish. The best part? The longer it sits in your fridge, the better it tastes, making it a great make-ahead meal!

SERVES 4 TO 6

PREP TIME: **20 minutes**
COOKING TIME: **20 minutes**
TOTAL TIME: **about 40 minutes, plus cooling time**

FOR THE DRESSING
½ cup avocado or sunflower oil
¼ cup red wine vinegar
2 tablespoons Classic Mayonnaise (page 42) or store-bought
1 tablespoon lemon juice
2 teaspoons Dijon mustard
2 teaspoons granulated sugar
½ teaspoon dried oregano
½ teaspoon kosher salt
¼ teaspoon dried basil
¼ teaspoon granulated garlic
¼ teaspoon onion powder
¼ teaspoon black pepper

FOR THE QUINOA SALAD
1 cup dry quinoa
1¾ cups water
½ teaspoon kosher salt
One 15-ounce can chickpeas, drained and rinsed
1 cup cherry or grape tomatoes, quartered
½ English cucumber, diced
½ cup crumbled feta cheese
10 pitted kalamata olives, halved lengthwise
¼ cup fresh parsley, chopped

1   To prepare the dressing: Add all the ingredients to a high-speed blender and blend until emulsified. Taste for seasoning and set aside. This dressing will last for up to a week stored in an airtight container in the refrigerator.

2   Next, prepare the quinoa. Pour the quinoa into a fine mesh strainer and rinse under cold running water to remove any bitterness on the outside, drain well.

3   Transfer the rinsed quinoa to a saucepan with the water and salt. Bring to a boil over medium-high heat. Then reduce to a light simmer. Cover and cook for 15 to 20 minutes, or until the quinoa is tender and has absorbed all the water.

4   Remove from the heat and let sit covered for another 5 minutes. Then remove the lid and fluff with a fork. Transfer to a large mixing bowl to cool.

5   Pour half of the dressing over the top of the quinoa—it's okay if it is a bit warm—and gently stir to combine. Let sit for about 10 minutes.

6   Add the remaining ingredients and stir to combine. Taste for seasoning and add more dressing if needed. This is a great make-ahead salad and will last for up to 5 days stored in an airtight container in the refrigerator.

KALE & CABBAGE CAESAR SALAD

Certain dishes are instant classics on our Feast & Fettle menu rotation, and our various takes on Caesar salad have quickly secured their status as favorites. For this rendition, we're elevating the classic by using a blend of baby kale and shredded red cabbage as our base. This creates a bold, peppery backdrop that pairs beautifully with the rich umami of Caesar dressing. While the recipe does call for the extra step of making homemade croutons, trust me, it's a game changer. Not only do they offer an improved flavor compared to their store-bought counterparts, but they also provide a delightful crunch that brings a necessary textural contrast to the dish.

SERVES 4

PREP TIME: 10 minutes
COOKING TIME: 20 minutes
TOTAL TIME: about 30 minutes

FOR THE DRESSING
½ cup Classic Mayonnaise (page 42) or store-bought
¼ cup sour cream
2 tablespoons grated Parmesan cheese
1 tablespoon whole milk, more if needed
1 teaspoon Dijon mustard
1 teaspoon Worcestershire sauce
½ to 1 teaspoon freshly cracked black pepper
½ teaspoon granulated garlic

FOR THE SALAD
½ loaf crusty bread, cut into ½- to 1-inch cubes
2 to 3 tablespoons extra virgin olive oil
½ teaspoon kosher salt
5 ounces baby kale
½ small head red cabbage, thinly shredded
½ cup grape tomatoes, halved lengthwise
½ cup shaved Parmesan cheese

1   To prepare the dressing: Add all the ingredients to a high-speed blender and blend, adding more milk if the dressing is too thick. Taste for seasoning and set aside. This dressing will last for up to a week stored in an airtight container in the refrigerator.

2   To prepare the salad: Heat the oven to 375°F. Line a rimmed baking sheet with parchment paper.

3   Toss the bread, oil, and salt in a large mixing bowl. Transfer the seasoned bread to the baking sheet and bake for 15 to 20 minutes, tossing halfway through, or until golden brown. Set aside to cool completely.

4   Add the kale and cabbage to a large mixing bowl with half of the dressing and toss to combine. Transfer to a large serving bowl and top with about 1 cup of the croutons, grape tomatoes, and Parmesan cheese, adding more dressing as needed. Serve immediately.

NOTE:

To make a classic Caesar salad, substitute 2 to 3 romaine lettuce hearts for the baby kale and red cabbage.

SOUTHWEST SALAD
with Creamy Cilantro Dressing

This salad has earned its lofty status as one of the most sought-after dishes at Feast & Fettle, and rightly so. Our version of this classic salad is substantial enough to double as an entrée with the addition of protein. While the mix of crisp lettuce, hearty beans, sweet corn, juicy tomatoes, creamy avocado, and crunchy tortilla chips bring a range of textures and flavors, it's the creamy cilantro dressing that transforms this dish from familiar to unforgettable. Featuring a slight kick from the jalapeño, a touch of sweetness from the honey, and the aromatic essence of cilantro leaves, this vibrant, creamy concoction does a fantastic job bringing all the components of the salad together.

SERVES 4 OR 5

TOTAL TIME: **about 15 minutes**

FOR THE DRESSING
½ **cup sour cream**
⅓ **cup fresh cilantro, chopped**
¼ **cup mayonnaise**
1 tablespoon lime juice
1 jalapeño, seeded and diced
1½ teaspoons kosher salt
2 garlic cloves, smashed
1 teaspoon honey
½ **teaspoon cumin**

FOR THE SALAD
2 to 3 romaine lettuce hearts, washed and chopped
One 15-ounce can black beans, drained and rinsed
⅓ **cup sweet corn kernels, fresh or frozen**
½ **cup shredded Monterey Jack cheese**
½ **cup cherry or grape tomatoes, halved lengthwise**
1 ripe avocado, sliced
½ **cup crushed corn tortilla chips**

1 To prepare the dressing: Add all the ingredients to a high-speed blender and blend, adding a little water if the dressing is too thick. Taste for seasoning and set aside. This dressing will last for up to a week stored in an airtight container in the refrigerator.

2 To assemble the salad: Add the lettuce, black beans, and corn to a large mixing bowl with half of the dressing and toss to combine. Transfer to a large serving bowl and top with the cheese, tomatoes, avocado, and tortilla chips. Drizzle with more dressing, if needed, and serve immediately.

SPINACH, BLUEBERRY & GOAT CHEESE SALAD

with Honey-Dijon Dressing

In New England, the arrival of the summer blueberry season is always a highlight, especially given that these flavorful berries are native to the region. In this salad, fresh blueberries take center stage nestled atop a base of tender baby spinach. Tangy goat cheese, pickled red onion, and the nuttiness of toasted almonds round out the flavors. The honey-Dijon dressing, with its creamy sweetness, ties everything together. It's a simple yet delicious way to celebrate the peak of blueberry season.

SERVES 4

TOTAL TIME: about 15 minutes

FOR THE DRESSING
½ cup avocado or sunflower oil
¼ cup apple cider vinegar
3 tablespoons Dijon mustard
3 tablespoons Classic Mayonnaise (page 42) or store-bought
1½ tablespoons honey
1 garlic clove, smashed
½ teaspoon kosher salt, more if needed

FOR THE SALAD
½ cup sliced almonds
8 ounces (6 to 7 cups) baby spinach
¾ cup fresh blueberries
¼ cup Easy Quick Pickled Red Onions (page 94)
⅓ cup crumbled goat cheese

1   To prepare the dressing: Add all the ingredients to a high-speed blender and blend until emulsified. Taste for seasoning and set aside. This dressing will last for up to a week stored in an airtight container in the refrigerator.

2   To prepare the salad: Preheat the oven to 325°F. Spread the almonds on a rimmed baking sheet. Roast for 8 minutes, or until lightly browned and fragrant.

3   Add the baby spinach and half of the blueberries to a large mixing bowl with about half of the dressing and toss to combine. Transfer to a large serving bowl and top with the remaining blueberries, pickled red onion, goat cheese, and toasted almonds, adding more dressing as needed. Serve immediately.

NOTES:

- You can substitute ¼ teaspoon of granulated garlic for 1 clove of garlic.
- You can substitute thinly sliced raw red onion for the pickled red onion.
- You can substitute feta cheese or shaved Parmesan for the goat cheese.

SUMMER PEACH & MOZZARELLA SALAD

with Sweet Vidalia Onion Dressing

Sun-kissed and bursting with flavor, a perfectly ripe peach captures the very essence of summer, inspiring this quintessential summer salad. Each bite melds the flavors and textures of ripe peaches and creamy mozzarella with the salty crunch of the roasted sunflower seeds. The star of this dish, however, is the dressing, with its mellow sweetness and subtle tartness and unexpected texture from the poppy seeds.

SERVES 4

TOTAL TIME: **about 15 minutes**

FOR THE DRESSING
½ **cup avocado or sunflower oil**
½ **cup sweet Vidalia onion, diced**
¼ **cup white wine vinegar**
¼ **cup granulated sugar**
½ **teaspoon kosher salt**
¼ **teaspoon mustard powder**
¼ **teaspoon ground turmeric**
2 **teaspoons poppy seeds**

FOR THE SALAD
8 **ounces (6 to 7 cups) baby crisp green lettuce**
1 **ripe peach, pitted and sliced**
¾ **cup fresh ciliegine mozzarella cheese, halved**
¼ **cup roasted and salted sunflower seeds**

1   To make the dressing: Add all the ingredients except for the poppy seeds to a high-speed blender and blend until emulsified. Add the poppy seeds and pulse a few times. Taste for seasoning and set aside. This dressing will last for up to 2 weeks stored in an airtight container in the refrigerator.

2   To assemble the salad: Add the lettuce and half of the peaches to a large mixing bowl with about half of the dressing and toss to combine. Top with the remaining peaches, mozzarella, and sunflower seeds, adding more dressing if needed. Serve immediately.

NOTE:

You can substitute any stone fruit, such as nectarine, apricot, plum, and so forth for the peach.

CHIVE POTATO SALAD

Getting potato salad just right can be a bit of a balancing act. While no one wants to bite into crunchy potatoes, serving potato salad reminiscent of mashed potatoes is equally undesirable. The trick is achieving potatoes that are tender throughout, with just a hint of crumble at the edges. This recipe pairs that perfect potato texture with a blend of tangy mayonnaise and Dijon mustard. The addition of chives offers a pop of freshness and a hint of oniony flair. It's a perfect dish for sharing at a backyard BBQ, or try pairing it with Juicy Turkey Burgers (page 29) for a relaxed weeknight dinner.

SERVES 6 TO 8

PREP TIME: 10 minutes
COOKING TIME: 12 minutes
TOTAL TIME: about 22 minutes, plus cooling

3 pounds Yukon Gold or yellow potatoes, peeled and cut into ¾-inch cubes

2 tablespoons plus 1 teaspoon kosher salt, more if needed

1 cup Classic Mayonnaise (page 42) or store-bought

1 tablespoon Dijon mustard

2 teaspoons fresh lemon juice

1 teaspoon white wine vinegar

½ teaspoon granulated garlic

¼ teaspoon ground black pepper, more if needed

2 tablespoons chives, thinly chopped

1 Add the potatoes to a large saucepan or pot with about 3 quarts of cold water and 2 tablespoons of salt. Set over medium-high heat and bring to a boil. Then reduce to a simmer and cook until fork tender, 12 to 15 minutes. Drain the potatoes in a colander and spread onto a rimmed baking sheet to cool to room temperature.

2 In a large mixing bowl, combine the mayonnaise, Dijon mustard, lemon juice, vinegar, garlic, pepper, and 1 teaspoon of salt, whisking together until smooth. Add the cooled potatoes and chives to the mayonnaise mixture and toss to combine. Taste for seasoning, adding more salt and pepper if needed. Refrigerate for at least 1 hour before serving. This is a great make-ahead salad and will last for up to a week stored in an airtight container in the refrigerator.

NOTE:

Feel free to use any medium-starch, all-purpose potato in this recipe.

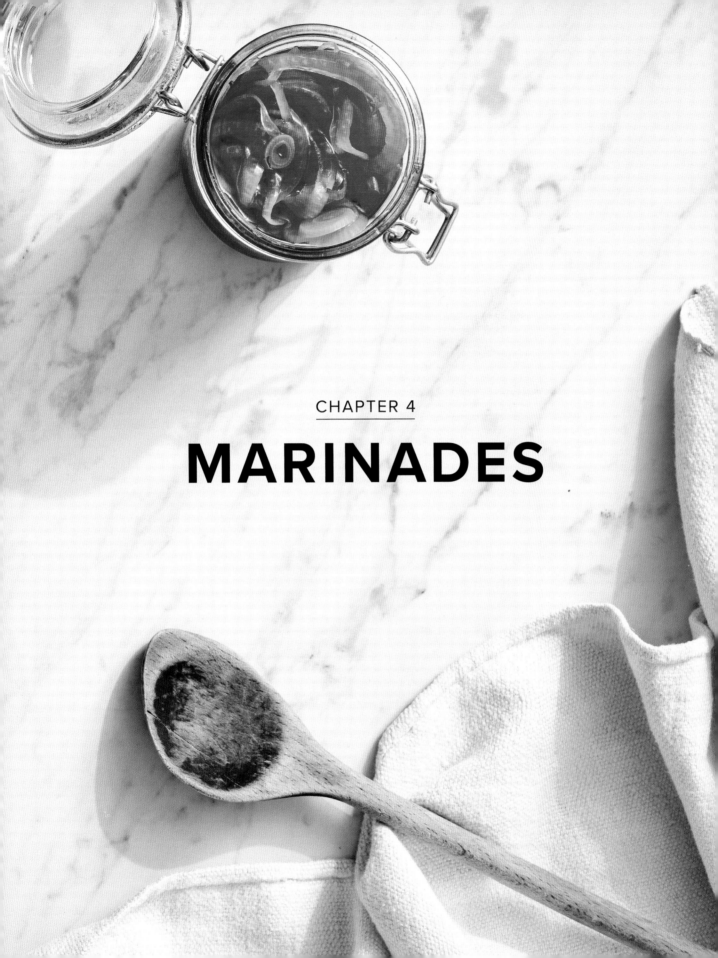

CHAPTER 4

MARINADES

With minimal effort and just a bit of patience, you can master the art of the marinade, a simple yet powerful technique that results in elevated flavor. A marinade is essentially a mixture of liquids and seasonings in which food is submerged. Its primary function is to season the surface of the food, and depending on the ingredients used and the food being marinated, it can also tenderize and add moisture to the dish.

The beauty of marinades is that they range from tangy and citrusy to sweet and spicy, offering endless possibilities to create unique and delicious flavor profiles. Once you've marinated your meat, fish, seafood, tofu, or veggies, there are various ways to finish off the dish, from grilling to oven roasting.

In this chapter, I expand the definition of marination to include brines and pickling liquids. Understanding the distinctions between these techniques is crucial, so let's dive right in. Salt and acid, two essential components that have been used for centuries to preserve and add flavor to food, are used for:

- *Brining is a technique that involves soaking food in a saltwater solution.* Salt plays a crucial role, because it helps break down the proteins in meat, fish, seafood, or vegetables, which allows for better absorption of liquid and other flavors into foods. The presence of salt in the brine also works to slow down the growth of bacteria, helping to preserve the food and prevent spoilage.
- *Marinating is a technique that involves soaking food in an acidic liquid, such as vinegar or citrus juice.* The acid adds a bright and tangy flavor and works to tenderize the food by breaking down its protein fibers. Acid can also help to preserve the food by inhibiting the growth of bacteria.
- *Pickling is a preservation technique that uses either salt or acid to both preserve foods and impart a sharp, sour, and salty taste.* The difference between salt pickling and traditional brining lies in the fermentation process. In salt pickling, the process is dominated by lactic acid bacteria. As fermentation progresses, the flavors deepen and become more tangy. On the other hand, pickling with acid, typically vinegar, results in quicker, unfermented pickles. The acid environment inhibits the growth of harmful microbes, preserving the food and delivering a pronounced tangy flavor.

It's important to note that some of these recipes require planning ahead. Marinating, brining, or pickling times can vary depending on the recipe. Some, like Chipotle Chili Lime Grilled Shrimp (page 96), require only 30 minutes of marination. Others, like Herbed Buttermilk Roasted Chicken Legs (page 99), need at least 6 hours of soaking time. Regardless, that time spent marinating is meant to create punchy, delicious flavors!

MARINATED RUBY RED BEETS

with Pomegranate Seeds

I think beets are beautiful. The inside colors are so rich and intense. But they are such a polarizing vegetable, with critics often eschewing their earthy flavor. Slow roasting whole beets completely transforms them: It brings out the complex natural sweetness of the roots and softens them to the perfect tender bite. The true highlight of this recipe is the pomegranate molasses, which has a sweet flavor but also delicious acidity. Adding the slow-roasted beets to the herbaceous sweet vinegar marinate infuses them with even more flavor. When serving this dish I like to toss the marinated beets with fresh, juicy pomegranate seeds for contrasting texture, as well as extra marinade and a touch of olive oil to give it a nice sheen.

SERVES 4 TO 6

PREP TIME: **10 minutes**
COOKING TIME: **1 hour 20 minutes**
MARINATING TIME: **1+ hours**
TOTAL TIME: **2 hours 30 minutes**

FOR THE MARINADE
1 cup pomegranate molasses
¾ cup balsamic vinegar
1-inch ginger knob, sliced
1 rosemary sprig
1 tablespoon kosher salt

FOR THE BEETS
2 pounds red beets, uniform in size, washed and trimmed
1 tablespoon extra virgin olive oil
1 teaspoon kosher salt
½ cup fresh pomegranate seeds

1   To make the marinade: Add the balsamic vinegar, pomegranate molasses, ginger, rosemary, and salt to a small saucepan and bring to a boil over high heat. Reduce heat to medium-low and simmer for 10 to 15 minutes to reduce and let the flavors infuse.

2   Take off the heat and strain the liquid using a fine mesh strainer into a small mixing bowl. Pour into a glass storage container and set aside to cool.

3   To prepare the beets: Adjust the oven rack to the middle position and heat to 400°F.

4   In a large mixing bowl, rub the beets with the olive oil and sprinkle with kosher salt.

5   Wrap each beet loosely with aluminum foil and place on a rimmed baking pan.

6   Bake for 50 to 70 minutes, depending on the size of the beets used. After about 40 minutes, check the beets in 10-minute intervals until tender. Beets are done when they can be easily pierced with a fork or cake tester.

7   Unwrap the beets from the foil and set aside until they are cool enough to handle. Hold one of the beets in your hand with a paper towel and start to rub the skin away; the skin should peel away easily. Repeat this process with all the beets. Once peeled you can rinse the beets under cool running water to help clean away any excess skin.

8 Cut the beets into bite-sized cubes or wedges and place in a mixing bowl. Pour the marinade mixture over the top of the warm beets, cover, and let sit in the refrigerator for at least 1 hour. The beets will last for up to 2 weeks in the marinade mixture.

9 To serve, remove the beets from the marinade and place in a shallow serving bowl, season with a pinch more salt, a drizzle of the leftover marinade, and then sprinkle with the pomegranate seeds.

NOTES:

- You can substitute cranberry juice concentrate for the pomegranate molasses, but the texture will not be as thick.
- I prefer the beets served cold, but you can easily warm them in the microwave for 1 to 2 minutes.

GRILLED MARINATED EGGPLANT

No one wants to get stuck cooking on a hot summer day! Make-ahead side dishes are a game changer, and this summer favorite of mine can be easily prepared ahead of time. What's more, the taste gets even better the longer it sits in the refrigerator. The lightly charred but tenderly grilled eggplant is perfectly complemented by the tangy, slightly spicy, herbaceous marinade, making for a truly delicious side dish. This recipe is versatile too—you can easily swap out the eggplant for other summer veggies such as bell peppers, onions, mushrooms, or broccoli.

SERVES 4 OR 5

PREP TIME: **5 minutes**
COOKING TIME: **5 minutes**
MARINATING TIME: **30 minutes**
TOTAL TIME: **about 40 minutes**

FOR THE MARINADE
½ **cup white balsamic vinegar**
¼ **cup extra virgin olive oil**
1 **large garlic clove, thinly sliced**
1 **teaspoon honey**
1 **teaspoon dried basil**
½ **teaspoon kosher salt**
½ **teaspoon crushed red pepper flakes**
½ **teaspoon dried thyme**

FOR THE EGGPLANT
2 **small Italian eggplants**
2 **tablespoons extra virgin olive oil**
1 **teaspoon kosher salt**

1   To make the marinade: Whisk all the ingredients together in a small mixing bowl and set aside.

2   To prepare the eggplant: Remove the stems from the eggplants and slice lengthwise into ¼-inch strips.

3   Allow the grill to preheat on a medium-high setting for about 5 minutes. Clean and oil the grilling grate.

4   Brush the eggplant with olive oil on both sides and season with salt. Grill for about 3 minutes per side, or until nice grill marks are achieved. Once the eggplant is tender, remove and place on a paper towel–lined plate to cool down a bit.

5   Add the eggplant to a large wide-mouth mason or glass jar. Pour the marinade mixture over the top of the eggplant, cover, and shake a bit to coat. Allow the eggplant to marinate for at least 30 minutes in the fridge before serving. This eggplant dish will last for up to 2 weeks stored in an airtight container in the refrigerator.

NOTES:

- The olive oil in the marinade may harden in the refrigerator; make sure to bring the dish to room temperature before serving.
- You can substitute any dried herb of your liking in place of the dried basil and thyme.
- Omit the crushed red pepper flakes if you want to avoid heat.

SWEET SOY GARLIC MARINATED PORTOBELLO MUSHROOMS

Portobello mushrooms boast a remarkable earthy flavor and a satisfying "meaty texture," making them a perfect choice for marinating and grilling. This recipe fully embraces the porous nature of mushrooms, a quality that allows them to readily absorb the umami-rich marinade, which in turn elevates their flavor profile before they hit the grill. While these mushrooms are undeniably great on their own, they truly shine when used as a patty in a vegetarian burger. I love to top mine with a dollop of Roasted Garlic Aioli (page 45), a juicy slice of fresh tomato, and crisp lettuce leaves, all nestled on a lightly toasted bun.

SERVES 4

PREP TIME: **5 minutes**
MARINATING TIME: **10+ minutes**
COOKING TIME: **15 minutes**
TOTAL TIME: **about 30 minutes**

FOR THE MARINADE
½ cup low-sodium soy sauce or tamari
⅓ cup light brown sugar
¼ cup water
¼ cup mirin
1 teaspoon toasted sesame oil
2 garlic cloves, minced

FOR THE MUSHROOMS
4 large portobello mushroom caps
2 tablespoons thinly sliced scallions

1 To make the marinade: Whisk together all the ingredients in a small saucepan. Bring mixture to a boil, then reduce to a simmer and let the sauce reduce and thicken slightly, 8 to 10 minutes. Set aside to cool.

2 To prepare the mushrooms: Gently twist the stems off the mushrooms and wipe down the tops of the mushrooms with a damp paper towel or rinse quickly under cold water. Use a spoon to gently scrape out the gills and discard.

3 Place the portobello mushroom caps in a square glass baking dish and pour the sweet soy garlic marinade over the top. Let the mushrooms sit in the marinade for at least 10 minutes but not longer than 30 minutes. During this time, make sure to flip them over in the marinade a few times.

4 Allow the grill to preheat on a medium-high setting for about 10 minutes. Clean and oil the grill grates.

5 Place the mushrooms, gill side down, onto the grill. Cook for 3 to 4 minutes or until browned and slightly tender. Flip the mushrooms over, brush with the remaining marinade, and let cook for another 2 to 3 minutes, or until browned and fully tender.

6 Transfer the mushrooms to a plate and sprinkle with the scallions to garnish.

NOTES:

- I always recommend removing the gills, as they can sometimes trap dirt or sand.
- Feel free to substitute the mushrooms with eggplant, zucchini, or any meat of your choice. Just remember that cooking times will differ.

EASY QUICK PICKLED RED ONIONS

At Feast & Fettle, one of our favorite ways to effortlessly enhance any dish is with the addition of pickled onions! We adore their sweet and tangy flavor, satisfying crunch, and striking pink hue. Unlike more traditional pickles that are shelf-stable, these pickled onions can be prepared quickly and then simply stored in the refrigerator. Their versatility truly knows no bounds. From adorning sandwiches to topping tacos, enhancing salads to serving as a tangy sidekick for an epic BBQ spread, pickled onions are the perfect way to add a zippy crunch to any dish.

MAKES ABOUT 3 CUPS

PREP TIME: **5 minutes**
COOKING TIME: **2 minutes**
MARINATING TIME: **2+ hours**
TOTAL TIME: **2 hours 7 minutes**

1 cup water

1 cup distilled white vinegar

2 tablespoons granulated sugar

2 teaspoons kosher salt

6 black peppercorns (optional)

1 bay leaf (optional)

1 garlic clove, smashed (optional)

1 medium red onion, peeled and
  thinly sliced

1   Bring the water, vinegar, sugar, salt, peppercorns, and bay leaf, if using, to a boil in a medium saucepan.

2   In the meantime, pack a 16-ounce glass jar with the garlic clove, if using, and the red onion.

3   Once the vinegar mixture starts boiling, turn off the heat and carefully pour the mixture over the top of the onions. Make sure the onions are fully submerged in the liquid, pressing down on them with the end of a wooden spoon if needed. Let sit on the counter until cool, then cover and place in the refrigerator for at least 2 hours or up to 3 weeks.

SWEET & SPICY BAKED TOFU

With its inherently neutral flavor, tofu can often be perceived as bland. However, by skillfully seasoning it with a complex, tangy marinade that incorporates a kick of Aleppo pepper, you can transform this versatile ingredient into a truly flavorful dish. The key to achieving amazing tofu texture is to press it. This removes excess water, creating a firmer texture on the inside as well as providing for a crispy exterior when cooked. In this recipe, once the tofu is pressed, marinated, and baked to crispy perfection, it is tossed in the reserved marinade to take the flavor to a whole new level! I suggest serving this tofu with herb-roasted baby potatoes and garlicky green beans.

SERVES 4

PREP TIME: **30 minutes (includes pressing time)**
MARINATING TIME: **30 minutes**
COOKING TIME: **30 minutes**
TOTAL TIME: **1 hour 30 minutes**

FOR THE MARINADE
¼ cup lemon juice, freshly squeezed
¼ cup extra virgin olive oil
¼ cup honey
3 tablespoons orange juice, freshly squeezed
2 tablespoons whole-grain mustard
1 teaspoon Aleppo pepper flakes
1 garlic clove, minced or grated
1 teaspoon granulated garlic
1 teaspoon dried oregano
1 teaspoon kosher salt

FOR THE TOFU
2 blocks (28 ounces) extra-firm tofu, drained

1 First make the marinade. In a medium mixing bowl, whisk together all the ingredients until the mixture is well combined.

2 Reserve half of the marinade for later.

3 To press the tofu: Place several layers of paper towels on a cutting board. Place the tofu on top of the paper towels and top with another several layers of paper towels. Place a cast-iron skillet or heavy-bottomed pan on top of the tofu and press for 20 to 30 minutes, or until enough water has drained to make a difference.

4 Cut the tofu into 1-inch slices, and then cut into 1-inch cubes. Add the tofu to the bowl with the marinade and gently toss to combine. Let marinate for about 30 minutes.

5 Adjust the oven rack to the middle position and preheat to 400°F.

6 Arrange the tofu in a single layer on a parchment paper–lined baking sheet. Bake for 15 minutes. Then gently flip the tofu over and bake for another 10 to 15 minutes, or until the tofu is lightly browned and crispy on the outside.

7 Transfer the baked tofu to a serving dish and drizzle the reserved marinade over the top and toss to combine.

NOTE:

You can substitute crushed red pepper flakes for the Aleppo pepper, but I would cut the amount in half as the crushed red pepper flakes are spicier than the Aleppo pepper.

CHIPOTLE CHILI LIME GRILLED SHRIMP

The flavors brought forth in this recipe are the perfect balance of smoky and tangy. The chipotle chili and lime juice brings the heat and tang, while the honey adds a touch of sweetness. The addition of cumin and fresh cilantro round out the flavor profile, making for a truly delicious and addictive dish. What's even better? The marinade doubles as a finishing sauce, ensuring that every bite of shrimp is bursting with flavor! While these shrimp are delicious all by themselves, they can also easily be incorporated into other dishes. Try them in a shrimp taco or on top of a Southwest Salad with Creamy Cilantro Dressing (page 76).

SERVES 4

PREP TIME: **10 minutes**
MARINATING TIME: **30 minutes**
COOKING TIME: **6 minutes**
TOTAL TIME: **about 46 minutes**

FOR THE MARINADE
1½ teaspoons pureed chipotle peppers in adobo
¼ cup fresh lime juice
2 tablespoons avocado or sunflower oil
1 tablespoon honey
½ teaspoon ground cumin
½ teaspoon kosher salt
2 tablespoons fresh cilantro, chopped

FOR THE SHRIMP
2 pounds raw jumbo shrimp (16 to 20 count), peeled and deveined

1 To make the chipotle puree: Add the entire can of chipotle peppers in adobo to a food processor fitted with an S blade and process until smooth. Store the unused portion in an airtight food storage container, which will last up to 7 days in the refrigerator or up to 6 months in the freezer.

2 To make the marinade: Combine the lime juice, oil, honey, chipotle puree, cumin, and salt in a medium bowl and whisk to emulsify. Then add the cilantro and whisk to combine.

3 Reserve 1 tablespoon of marinade to use as a finishing sauce and set the rest of the marinade aside.

4 Next, prepare the shrimp. Make sure the shrimp are fairly dry, using a paper towel to blot off any excess moisture.

5 Add the shrimp to the bowl with the marinade and place in the refrigerator for up to 30 minutes.

6 Allow the grill to preheat on a medium-high setting for about 10 minutes. Clean and oil the grilling grate.

7 Place the shrimp on the hot grill and cook until they have turned opaque and are cooked through, 2 to 3 minutes per side.

8 Transfer the shrimp to a bowl and toss with reserved marinade. Taste for seasoning and serve immediately.

NOTES:

- You can store the chipotle puree in ice cube trays and, once frozen, add to a zip-lock bag to use as needed.

- You can leave the tails on the shrimp or take them off prior to marinating, it's a personal preference—I typically leave the tails on.

- I do not recommend marinating the shrimp for longer than an hour, because the acidic ingredients in the marinade will begin to negatively affect the texture of the shrimp.

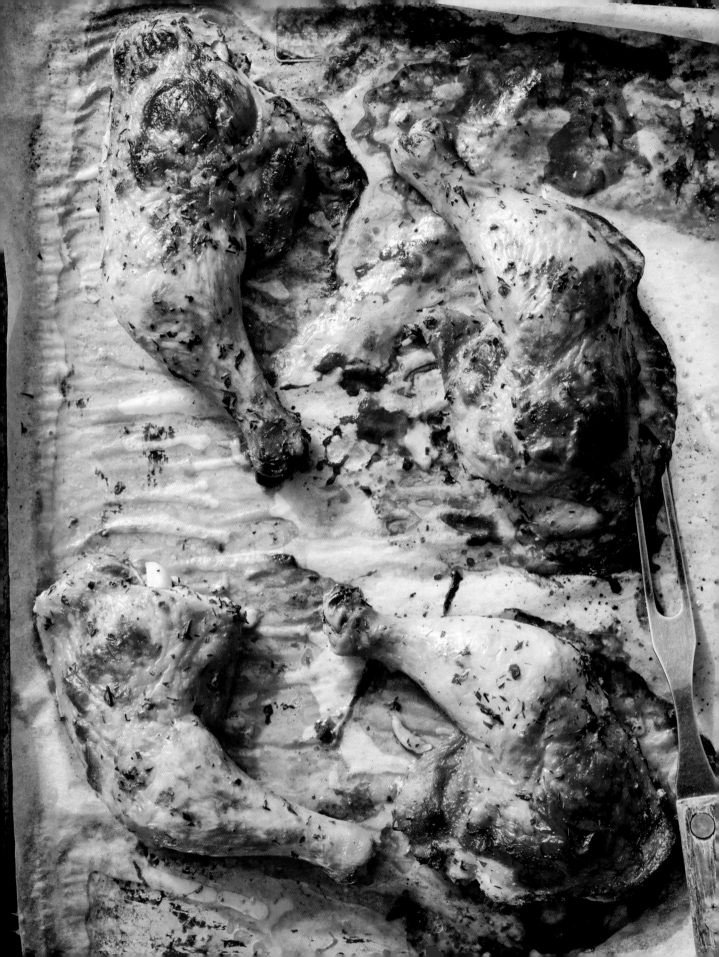

HERBED BUTTERMILK ROASTED CHICKEN LEGS

Cooking chicken well can be challenging—it often comes out bland and dry. But don't underestimate the power of a brine. Taking the time to brine your chicken can be a game changer, resulting in incredibly flavorful and juicy meat. This recipe combines buttermilk, citrus, fresh herbs, garlic, salt, and pepper to create a unique blend of marinade and brine. Buttermilk's natural acidity, thanks to the presence of lactic acid, starts to tenderize the chicken while the salt acts as a brine, penetrating multiple layers of the meat. The citrus, fresh herbs, and garlic, on the other hand, flavor the surface of the chicken, much like a marinade, adding an extra layer of complexity to the dish.

SERVES 4

PREP TIME: **10 minutes**
MARINATING TIME: **12+ hours**
COOKING TIME: **40 minutes**
TOTAL TIME: **12 hours 50 minutes**

FOR THE MARINADE
2 cups buttermilk
1 teaspoon lemon zest
1 tablespoon fresh thyme, finely chopped
1 tablespoon fresh rosemary, finely chopped
3 to 4 teaspoons kosher salt
1 tablespoon fresh lemon juice
1 teaspoon ground black pepper
2 teaspoons fresh parsley, finely chopped
2 garlic cloves, smashed

FOR THE CHICKEN
4 whole chicken legs, drumstick and thigh
1 to 2 tablespoons extra virgin olive oil

1 To make the marinade: Add all the ingredients to a medium mixing bowl and whisk to combine.

2 Next, prepare the chicken. Open and place a gallon-size resealable freezer bag in a large mixing bowl; add the chicken legs to the bag.

3 Pour the buttermilk mixture over the top of the chicken legs. Seal the bag while pressing out as much air as possible. Mix around the chicken in the bag so that the buttermilk brine is evenly distributed.

4 Transfer to the refrigerator and let sit for at least 12 hours or up to 24 hours.

5 Adjust the oven rack to the middle position and heat to 425°F. Line a rimmed baking sheet with parchment paper.

6 Remove the chicken legs from the brine, shaking them to remove any excess buttermilk mixture, and place the chicken skin side up onto the baking sheet.

7 Roast the chicken for about 25 minutes. Then brush the skin with the olive oil and roast for another 10 to 15 minutes, or until the skin is crisp and deeply browned and the internal temperature reaches 155° to 160°F on an instant-read thermometer.

8 Allow the chicken to rest for 5 minutes before serving.

NOTE:

If excess liquid accumulates on the sheet pan during the roasting process, just carefully pour it off before brushing the skin with olive oil.

APPLE CIDER BRINED PORK CHOPS

Apples and pork are a timeless pairing. In this recipe, apple cider is used to combat pork's tendency toward dryness. Plan ahead: These pork chops soak in a brine of fresh apple cider for at least six hours, which infuses them with sweet and savory flavor and ensures tenderness and juiciness during the cooking process. Following the brine, the chops are reverse seared, which is a cooking method that promises a moist final product. The chops are gently cooked in the oven until they hit just the right internal temperature. They're then finished in a sizzling hot pan, basted with butter until beautifully browned. The outcome is a supremely succulent pork chop that pairs perfectly with the Apple & Shaved Fennel Salad with Apple Cider Vinaigrette (page 68) and a side of creamy mashed potatoes.

SERVES 4

PREP TIME: **5 minutes**
MARINATING TIME: **6+ hours**
COOKING TIME: **40 minutes**
TOTAL TIME: **6 hours 45 minutes**

FOR THE BRINE
¾ cup fresh apple cider
1 cup water
2 tablespoons brown sugar
2 tablespoons kosher salt
8 whole black peppercorns
1 garlic clove, smashed
1 stem fresh rosemary
1 bay leaf

FOR THE PORK
4 bone-in pork chops, about 1 inch thick
Kosher salt, as needed
Ground black pepper, as needed
1 tablespoon avocado or sunflower oil
1 tablespoon salted butter

NOTES:

- Feel free to substitute boneless pork chops for the bone-in pork chops.
- Add a few ice cubes to the brine if you want to cool it down faster.

1 First, make the brine. In a small saucepan, bring the apple cider, water, brown sugar, salt, peppercorns, and garlic to boil. Reduce to a simmer and whisk until both the sugar and salt are dissolved. Add the rosemary and bay leaf and turn off the heat; this should take about 3 minutes total. Remove the brine from the stove and **allow it to cool completely** before using.

2 Next, add the pork chops to a large zip-lock bag or place in a large bowl, pour the cooled brine over the chops, seal or cover, and refrigerate for at least 6 hours or up to 24 hrs.

3 Adjust the oven rack to the middle position and preheat to 300°F.

4 Take the pork chops out of the brine and dry with paper towels. Season the pork chops on both sides with a pinch more salt and pepper and place on a wire rack set inside a rimmed baking sheet lined with aluminum foil.

5 Place the baking sheet in the oven and cook the pork chops for 20 to 25 minutes, or until the internal temperature reaches 110° to 115°F on an instant-read thermometer.

6 Heat the oil in a cast-iron or stainless steel skillet over medium-high until shimmering. Place the pork chops in the skillet two at a time, sear until well browned on one side, 2 to 3 minutes, then flip the chops. Add the butter to the pan, tilt the pan to one side, and use a large spoon to continuously baste the foamy butter over the top of the pork chops; this should take another 3 minutes. The pork is done when the internal temperature reaches 135°F on an instant-read thermometer.

GREEK CHICKEN SOUVLAKI SKEWERS

Skewered chicken is a summer classic, but it's all too easy to end up with a dry and over-cooked dish. However, in this interpretation of souvlaki, which translates to "meat on a skewer," we're taking things up a notch by marinating the chicken thighs in a flavorful combination of red wine vinegar, lemon juice, garlic, and herbs that not only infuses flavor onto the surface of the meat but also tenderizes it. This results in a dish that's juicy and flavorful every time. What's more, these skewers are baked, not grilled, so you can enjoy them year-round! I suggest serving them with a side of homemade Tzatziki Sauce (page 53), warm pita, and an easy salad of juicy tomatoes and cucumbers drizzled with good olive oil and a splash of red wine vinegar.

SERVES 4

PREP TIME: **20 minutes**
MARINATING TIME: **30+ minutes**
COOKING TIME: **20 minutes**
TOTAL TIME: **1 hour 10 minutes**

FOR THE MARINADE
½ cup extra virgin olive oil
¼ cup red wine vinegar
2 tablespoons lemon juice
3 garlic cloves, smashed
2 teaspoons dry oregano
1 teaspoon dried basil
1 teaspoon kosher salt
½ teaspoon black pepper

FOR THE CHICKEN SKEWERS
2 pounds chicken thighs, boneless and skinless, cut into even 1-inch chunks
8 to 10 wooden skewers, soaked in water
½ to 1 teaspoon kosher salt

1 To make the marinade: Add all the marinade ingredients to a medium mixing bowl and whisk until combined.

2 To prepare the chicken: Add the thighs to a large zip-lock bag and pour the marinade over the top. Seal the bag, massage the marinade around the chicken, and refrigerate for at least 30 minutes or up to 24 hours.

3 Adjust the oven rack to the highest position and set to broil (high).

4 Thread the chicken evenly onto the soaked wooden skewers, you want the chicken piece to be touching each other, and place on a wire rack set inside a rimmed baking sheet lined with aluminum foil. Sprinkle the salt over the prepared chicken skewers.

5 Broil for 5 to 8 minutes, then flip the skewers over and broil for another 5 minutes, or until nicely browned and the internal temperature reaches 155°F on an instant-read thermometer. Loosely cover the skewers with aluminum foil and let rest for 3 to 5 minutes before serving.

NOTES:

• This recipe will work just as well with boneless, skinless chicken breasts or pork tenderloin.

• If a lot of liquid accumulates during the roasting process, just pour some of it off during the broiling process.

• Alternatively, you can grill the skewers over high heat for about 6 minutes per side. Make sure to oil the grill grates before adding the skewers.

CHAPTER 5

COMPOUND BUTTERS

Butter, the creamy and luscious staple we all know and love, holds endless possibilities when combined with herbs, spices, and other flavorful ingredients. It's worth noting that whenever I mention butter in this chapter, I'm referring to American butter, available in both salted and unsalted varieties, with a butterfat content of 80 percent.

Compound butter is a simple yet transformative concoction that effortlessly elevates ordinary dishes to extraordinary levels of flavor while also adding a bit of decadence. At Feast & Fettle, we frequently enhance our menu items with delicious compound butters. We have discovered that this is an excellent method to infuse our dishes with both complexity and richness. In this chapter, you will find a few recipes that have become popular Feast & Fettle dishes, such as Bucatini with Cacio e Pepe Butter (page 109) or Grilled Shrimp with Herb Scampi Butter (page 117). You will also find some bold and innovative recipes that showcase the versatility of compound butter, such as Sautéed Snap Peas with Kimchi-Miso Butter (page 113).

Although the technique of making compound butter is simple, these tips will help you streamline the process:

- Softening the butter is *key*. The best method is to let it sit at room temperature for about an hour. If time is limited, there's a handy shortcut: Simply slice or cube the butter and spread the pieces on a plate without overlapping. This increases the surface area and helps the butter to come to room temperature in about 15 minutes.
- Rolling the compound butter into a log shape and tightly wrapping it in parchment paper or plastic wrap before chilling in the refrigerator allows the butter to solidify while infusing it with maximum flavor. This also makes it convenient to store any extra compound butter in the refrigerator or freezer for later use.
- If you don't want to roll the compound butter, you can simply scoop the butter mixture into a glass jar to store in the refrigerator.

Having compound butter on hand is a true kitchen luxury, as it allows you to effortlessly create indulgent weekday meals with ease.

BUCATINI WITH CACIO E PEPE BUTTER

Traditional Italian cacio e pepe, known for its simplicity and bold flavors, is typically made with just three ingredients: Pecorino Romano cheese, black peppercorns, and pasta. At Feast & Fettle, we put our own spin on this classic dish by introducing a flavorful compound butter, with all the flavors you would expect in a traditional cacio e pepe. The star of our cacio e pepe butter is the freshly cracked black pepper, which lends a robust and aromatic punch to every bite. With the compound butter prepared ahead of time, creating this dish becomes a true breeze. The richness of this pasta calls for a refreshing side dish. Serving it alongside a crunchy green salad, such as our Apple & Shaved Fennel Salad with Apple Cider Vinaigrette (page 68), adds a delightful contrast.

SERVES 2 TO 4

PREP TIME: **10 minutes**
COOKING TIME: **15 minutes**
TOTAL TIME: **about 25 minutes, plus chilling time**

FOR THE BUTTER

- **½ cup unsalted butter, softened**
- **⅓ cup finely grated Pecorino Romano cheese**
- **¼ cup finely grated Parmigiano-Reggiano cheese**
- **1 tablespoon freshly cracked black pepper**
- **¼ teaspoon kosher salt**

FOR THE PASTA

- **1 pound dried bucatini**
- **1 tablespoon kosher salt**
- **2 tablespoons grated Pecorino Romano cheese**

1 To make the butter: Add all the ingredients to the bowl of a stand mixer fitted with the paddle attachment. Beat the mixture on medium-high speed until fully combined.

2 Scoop the butter onto a piece of parchment paper, forming a line about 4 inches long, then wrap and roll into a log shape, twisting the ends to close.

3 Chill in the refrigerator for at least 2 hours before slicing. The butter will last for up to a week in the refrigerator or up to 3 months in the freezer.

4 To make the pasta: Bring a large pot with about 4 quarts of cold water to a boil, adding the salt to the water.

5 Add the bucatini and cook until al dente, 9 to 12 minutes depending on the brand you are using. Reserve 1 to 2 tablespoons of the pasta water before draining.

6 Add half of the cacio e pepe butter to the pot, then add the hot pasta over the top of the butter. Toss well, adding a little of the reserved pasta water as necessary to create a bit of a sauce. Top the pasta with the grated Pecorino Romano cheese and serve immediately.

NOTE:

To achieve the perfect balance of cheesy goodness, you will want to freshly grate the Pecorino Romano and Parmigiano-Reggiano cheeses using a cheese grater. While pre-grated cheeses are convenient, to prevent clumping they often contain additives that we want to avoid in this recipe.

ROASTED ROOT VEGETABLES
with Blue Cheese Butter

Once the fall season hits New England and the weather begins to cool, I get excited to see an abundance of root vegetables at my local market. Although roasted root vegetables are delicious on their own, adding this blue cheese butter over the top of the warm vegetables instantly takes this dish to the next level. Salty, tangy blue cheese is the perfect complement to the natural sweetness from the roasted vegetables. This recipe is extremely versatile, so feel free to use whichever root vegetables you like best or ones that are available in your area.

SERVES 4 OR 5

PREP TIME: **15 minutes**
COOKING TIME: **50 minutes**
TOTAL TIME: **about 1 hour 5 minutes,** plus chilling time

FOR THE BUTTER
1 stick (8 tablespoons) unsalted butter, softened
2 to 3 tablespoons blue cheese crumbles
1 teaspoon finely sliced chives
½ teaspoon kosher salt

FOR THE VEGETABLES
1 pound sweet potatoes, peeled and cut into 1-inch cubes
1 pound carrots, peeled and cut into 1-inch cubes
½ pound parsnips, peeled and cut into 1-inch cubes
3 tablespoons extra virgin olive oil
1 teaspoon kosher salt
¼ teaspoon ground black pepper

1   To make the butter: Add all the ingredients to the bowl of a stand mixer fitted with the paddle attachment. Beat the mixture on medium-high speed until fully combined.

2   Scoop the butter onto a piece of parchment paper, forming a line about 4 inches long, then wrap and roll into a log shape, twisting the ends to close.

3   Chill in the refrigerator for at least 2 hours before slicing. The butter will last for up to a week in the refrigerator or up to 3 months in the freezer.

4   To prepare the veggies: Heat the oven to 425°F and brush a rimmed baking sheet with olive oil.

5   In a large mixing bowl, toss all the vegetables together with the olive oil, salt, and pepper until well coated.

6   Add the vegetables to the baking sheet and roast in the oven for 40 to 50 minutes, or until tender and golden brown. Turn the vegetables over with a spatula after about 30 minutes.

7   Once out of the oven, let the vegetables cool slightly for about 5 minutes, then add a few thick slices of the blue cheese butter around the baking sheet. Once the butter has melted, lightly toss vegetables to coat and serve immediately.

NOTE:

You can substitute any hard squash, potatoes, beets, or turnips for any of the root vegetables used in this recipe.

SAUTÉED SNAP PEAS
with Kimchi-Miso Butter

Blanching is the secret to preserving the vibrant color, crisp texture, and essential nutrients of vegetables. Prior to sautéing, this recipe calls for blanching the snap peas in boiling salted water and then transferring them to an ice water bath. This simple yet crucial step ensures that the snap peas retain their natural sweetness and vibrant green color. This dish is finished by sautéing the snap peas in a rich compound butter infused with the spicy, umami-packed flavors of kimchi and the salty-sweetness of miso. These sautéed snap peas pair wonderfully with steamed jasmine rice, as the flavors of the butter beautifully season the rice as well.

SERVES 4

PREP TIME: **10 minutes**
COOKING TIME: **2 minutes**
TOTAL TIME: **about 12 minutes, plus chilling time**

FOR THE BUTTER
1 stick (8 tablespoons) unsalted butter, softened
2 tablespoons drained and chopped kimchi
1 teaspoon white miso
1 teaspoon thinly sliced scallions
¼ teaspoon kosher salt

FOR THE SNAP PEAS
1 pound snap peas, trimmed or stringless
1 tablespoon kosher salt
1 tablespoon thinly sliced scallions

1   To make the butter: Add all the ingredients to the bowl of a stand mixer fitted with the paddle attachment. Beat the mixture on medium-high speed until fully combined.

2   Scoop the butter onto a piece of parchment paper, forming a line about 4 inches long, then wrap and roll into a log shape, twisting the ends to close.

3   Chill in the refrigerator for at least 2 hours before slicing. The butter will last for up to a week in the refrigerator or up to 3 months in the freezer.

4   To prepare the snap peas: Bring a large pot of water to boil, adding the salt to the water. While the water is coming to a boil, fill a medium mixing bowl halfway full with ice and water and set aside.

5   Add the snap peas to the boiling water, making sure they are fully submerged. Cook for 1 to 2 minutes, or until the snap peas are just tender. Remove the peas with a slotted spoon or spider strainer, or pour into a colander and immediately submerge in the ice water bath.

6   Once the ice has melted, drain into a colander and place the snap peas onto a paper towel–lined plate to dry.

7   Melt half of the kimchi-miso butter in a large skillet over medium heat. Add the snap peas to the melted butter and toss well to coat. Pour the snap peas into a serving bowl and garnish with the scallions. Serve immediately.

NOTE:

This recipe also works beautifully with green beans or broccoli; just increase the cooking time to 3 to 4 minutes.

STEAMED FRESH CORN

with Chipotle-Honey Butter

Fresh corn is undoubtedly one of my all-time favorite summer vegetables! While it's no surprise that butter is a common companion to corn, in this case, the extra effort of making compound butter is absolutely worthwhile. The combination of smoky and spicy chipotle chilies, along with the sweetness of the honey-infused butter, creates a delightful contrast that elevates the natural sweetness in the corn. This dish complements a wide range of grilled entrées, but I particularly enjoy it alongside Grilled Flank Steak with Sweet Basil Chimichurri Sauce (page 133) or served alongside Grilled Chicken Fajitas (page 181).

SERVES 4

PREP TIME: **15 minutes**
COOKING TIME: **5 minutes**
TOTAL TIME: **about 20 minutes, plus chilling time**

FOR THE BUTTER
1 teaspoon pureed chipotle peppers in adobo
1 stick (8 tablespoons) unsalted butter, softened
1 tablespoon honey
1 teaspoon kosher salt

FOR THE CORN
4 large ears of corn, husks and silks removed

NOTES:

- This recipe also works well with steamed broccoli or green beans.
- To pick the best corn, there are a few tricks to keep in mind. Seek out the freshest corn possible, preferably from a local farm stand or farmers' market, as corn loses moisture rapidly after picking. Look for bright green husks and ears that feel heavy in your hand. Lastly, peel back a bit of the husk and look for tight rows of plump corn kernels.

1 To make the chipotle puree: Add the entire can of chipotle peppers in adobo to a food processor fitted with an S blade and process until smooth. Reserve 1 teaspoon and add the unused puree to an airtight food storage container, which will last up to 7 days in the refrigerator or up to 6 months in the freezer.

2 To make the butter: Add the reserved chipotle and all the remaining ingredients to the bowl of a stand mixer fitted with the paddle attachment. Beat the mixture on medium-high speed until fully combined.

3 Scoop the butter onto a piece of parchment paper, forming a line about 4 inches long, then wrap and roll into a log shape, twisting the ends to close.

4 Chill in the refrigerator for at least 2 hours before slicing. The butter will last for up to a week in the refrigerator or up to 3 months in the freezer.

5 To prepare the corn: Add just enough water to fill the base of a large pot then place a vegetable steamer over the water, cover, and bring to a boil. Once the water is boiling, add the corn to the steamer and cook for 4 to 5 minutes, or until the corn is tender and bright yellow.

6 Remove the corn from the steamer with tongs and place on a paper towel–lined plate to drain.

7 Rub a slice of the chipotle-honey butter over each warm corncob and serve immediately.

GRILLED SHRIMP
with Herb Scampi Butter

The inspiration behind this Feast & Fettle favorite was to create a lighter yet incredibly satisfying version of the beloved classic pasta dish: shrimp scampi. Here, we've captured all the irresistible flavors that define shrimp scampi, such as garlic, lemon, and parsley, and combine them into a sensational herb-infused scampi butter. Even better, this dish can be prepared ahead of time, making it incredibly convenient for busy weekday nights. Simply grill up your shrimp and toss them with the premade butter, effortlessly combining the smoky flavors of the grill with the herb-infused richness of the scampi butter.

SERVES 4

PREP TIME: **10 minutes**
MARINATING TIME: **15 minutes**
COOKING TIME: **5 minutes**
TOTAL TIME: **about 20 minutes, plus chilling time**

FOR THE BUTTER
1 stick (8 tablespoons) unsalted butter, softened
3 garlic cloves, minced
1 tablespoon fresh parsley, finely chopped
2 teaspoons lemon zest
1 teaspoon dried oregano
¼ teaspoon crushed red pepper flakes
½ teaspoon kosher salt, more if needed

FOR THE SHRIMP
2 pounds raw jumbo shrimp (16 to 20 count), peeled and deveined
¼ cup white wine
2 tablespoons avocado or sunflower oil
1 teaspoon kosher salt

1   To make the butter: Add all the ingredients to the bowl of a stand mixer fitted with the paddle attachment, and beat on medium-high speed until fully combined.

2   Scoop the butter onto a piece of parchment paper, forming a line about 4 inches long, then wrap and roll into a log shape, twisting the ends to close.

3   Chill in the refrigerator for at least 2 hours before slicing. The butter will last for up to a week in the refrigerator or up to 3 months in the freezer.

4   To prepare the shrimp: Make sure the shrimp are fairly dry, using a paper towel to blot off any excess moisture.

5   Add the shrimp to a mixing bowl with the wine, oil, and salt and toss to combine. Place in the refrigerator and let marinate for about 15 minutes.

6   While the shrimp are marinating, allow the grill to preheat on medium-high for about 10 minutes. Clean and oil the grilling grates.

7   Place the shrimp on the hot grill, turning occasionally until the shrimp have turned opaque or are no longer transparent, about 2 minutes per side. They should be just cooked through and have a bit of char on the outside.

8   Transfer the shrimp to a serving bowl and top with half of the herb scampi butter; lightly toss to allow the warm shrimp to melt the butter. Taste for seasoning and serve immediately.

NOTE:

For a sweeter garlic flavor, roast the garlic before adding it to the butter.

GRILLED SUMMER SWORDFISH

with Sun-Dried Tomato Butter

When it comes to grilling, not all fish can handle the heat. Some are too delicate for the grill, but not swordfish. Standing out with its firm and lean flesh, mild flavor, and dense steak-like texture, swordfish provides the perfect foundation for bold flavors. This vibrant and herbaceous sun-dried tomato compound butter was made for grilled swordfish. Due to the richness of the butter, I find that the swordfish pairs exceptionally well with simple grilled asparagus, or a refreshing side salad like Spinach, Blueberry & Goat Cheese Salad with Honey-Dijon Dressing (page 79).

SERVES 4

PREP TIME: **10 minutes**
COOKING TIME: **10 minutes**
TOTAL TIME: **about 20 minutes, plus chilling time**

FOR THE BUTTER

1 stick (8 tablespoons) unsalted butter, softened
⅓ cup sun-dried tomatoes, finely chopped
1 tablespoon fresh parsley, finely chopped
1 garlic clove, minced
½ teaspoon dried basil
½ teaspoon kosher salt

FOR THE FISH

4 center-cut swordfish steaks, about 6 ounces each, 1 inch thick
1 tablespoon avocado or sunflower oil, or any neutral oil
1 teaspoon kosher salt
¼ teaspoon ground black pepper

1   To make the butter: Add all the ingredients to the bowl of a stand mixer fitted with the paddle attachment. Beat the mixture on medium-high speed until fully combined.

2   Scoop the butter onto a piece of parchment paper, forming a line about 4 inches long, then wrap and roll into a log shape, twisting the ends to close.

3   Chill in the refrigerator for at least 2 hours before slicing. The butter will last for up to a week in the refrigerator or up to 3 months in the freezer.

4   To prepare the fish: Dry the swordfish steaks well with paper towels. Place the swordfish steaks on a plate, brush both sides with the oil, and season with salt and pepper.

5   Allow the grill to preheat on medium-high for about 10 minutes. Clean and oil the grilling grate.

6   Place the swordfish steaks on the grill, cover, and cook for about 5 minutes, or until the fish releases easily from the grill. Flip and cook for another 3 minutes or until an instant-read thermometer reaches 130°F for medium, 135°F for medium-well, or 140°F for well done.

7   Transfer the swordfish to a plate and place one ½-inch-thick slice of the sun-dried tomato butter on each piece. Serve once the butter is slightly melted over the fish.

NOTE:

Ahi tuna, salmon, or mahi-mahi can be substituted for the swordfish steaks in this recipe, as these fish hold up well to the grill.

REVERSE SEARED FILET MIGNON

with Roasted Garlic Butter

Filet mignon is the epitome of decadence. This cut is renowned for its melt-in-your-mouth tenderness and delicate favor. To ensure the best possible outcome, I recommend reverse searing, a technique that slowly cooks the steak to perfection. This method guarantees even cooking from edge to edge, resulting in optimal tenderness. The infused sweet nuttiness of the roasted garlic butter accentuates the natural flavor of the meat, elevating its already exceptional flavor. This recipe is an ideal choice for a special occasion. To complete the meal, I recommend serving it alongside roasted baby potatoes and Kale & Cabbage Caesar Salad (page 75).

SERVES 2, ABOUT 7 OUNCES PER SERVING

PREP TIME: **10 minutes**
COOKING TIME: **1 hour 20 minutes**
TOTAL TIME: **about 1 hour 30 minutes, plus chilling time**

FOR THE BUTTER
1 garlic bulb
1 to 2 teaspoons extra virgin olive oil
1 stick (8 tablespoons) unsalted butter, softened
1 teaspoon fresh parsley, finely chopped
1 teaspoon kosher salt

FOR THE STEAK
2 filets mignons, 7 to 8 ounces each, 1½ inches thick
1 teaspoon kosher salt
1 teaspoon avocado or sunflower oil

1   To make the butter: Preheat the oven to 400°F.

2   Peel off most of the loose, papery outer layers around the garlic bulb, while leaving the head intact. Slice off the top of the garlic bulb, exposing the tops of the cloves. Place the garlic bulb on top of a piece of aluminum foil, then drizzle with the olive oil and wrap tightly.

3   Roast in the oven for 40 to 50 minutes depending on the size of the garlic bulb. Start testing it after about 40 minutes; when done the center clove should be completely soft and easy to pierce with a toothpick or knife. Once cool, press or squeeze the bottom of the garlic bulb to push the cloves out of the paper. Set the roasted garlic cloves aside.

4   Add the butter, parsley, and salt to the bowl of a stand mixer fitted with the paddle attachment. Beat the mixture on medium-high speed until fully combined.

5   Scoop the butter onto a piece of parchment paper, forming a line about 4 inches long, then wrap and roll into a log shape, twisting the ends to close.

6   Chill in the refrigerator for at least 2 hours before slicing. The butter will last for up to a week in the refrigerator or up to 3 months in the freezer.

7   To prepare the steaks: Preheat the oven to 200°F.

8   Season the filet mignon steaks with salt on both sides and place on a rack set inside a sheet pan. Roast in the oven until an internal temperature of 120°F is reached on an instant-read thermometer, about 30 minutes (start checking the temperature after 25 minutes).

Remove the steaks from the oven and let rest on a paper towel–lined plate for about 10 minutes.

9 Add the oil to a cast-iron skillet over high heat; the pan is hot enough once the oil begins to smoke.

10 Sear the steaks on each side for 1 to 2 minutes, or until deeply browned on both sides. Transfer to a plate and let rest for 2 minutes before placing a ½-inch-thick slice of roasted garlic butter on top of each of the steaks. Serve immediately.

NOTES:

- This recipe will work with rib eye steak or New York strip steak, as long as they are cut at least 1½ inches thick.

- It's important to select even, lightly marbled filet mignon steaks, as you want them to cook at the same rate.

CHAPTER 6

SAUCES

At Feast & Fettle, we take our sauces seriously! You can see it across our menu selections. For us, the sauce isn't an afterthought; it's the costar. While many home cooks might skip this step, the secret to an unforgettable meal often lies in its sauce. Roasted Rack of Lamb with Cherry Port Sauce (page 137) is a standout example. The sauce masterfully balances the sweetness of the cherries and port wine with the tang from the balsamic vinegar, ensuring the lamb's richness is highlighted, not overshadowed.

Celebrated for elevating flavors, adding visual appeal, and introducing delightful textures, sauces are foundational to a cook's culinary arsenal, transforming dishes from simple to spectacular. Take, for instance, Grilled Flank Steak with Sweet Basil Chimichurri Sauce (page 133). With its herbaceous and vinegary notes, the chimichurri not only adds flavor and moisture to the steak but also introduces contrasting texture and color, taking a basic steak recipe to another level.

Diving in to the chapter, you'll discover that sauces bring a world of possibilities to everyday cooking and can be utilized in a variety of ways:

- Sauces can be elegantly served on the side, as with the Herb-Crusted Pork Tenderloin with Fresh Cranberry Sauce (page 138)
- Sauces can be used as a glaze to infuse flavors directly onto the main ingredients, as evidenced in the Brown Sugar Mustard-Glazed Holiday Ham (page 134)
- Sauces can serve as the medium in which ingredients are tossed, like in Fresh Udon Noodles with Creamy Peanut Sauce (page 129)

Many of the sauces featured in this chapter can be prepared ahead of time, significantly reducing your overall cooking time.

BLANCHED BROCCOLINI

with Roasted Red Pepper Sauce

I'm a big fan of blanching vegetables, and after trying this recipe, you might be too! Blanching is a cooking technique in which you briefly immerse vegetables in salted boiling water, then give them a quick shock in ice water to stop the cooking process. The result? Stunningly vibrant green veggies that are tender yet still pack a bit of crunch. The subtle flavor of blanched broccolini—seasoned only by the salted water—beautifully complements the smoky, sweet, lively notes of this roasted red pepper sauce.

SERVES 4

PREP TIME: **15 minutes**
COOKING TIME: **5 minutes**
TOTAL TIME: **about 20 minutes**

FOR THE SAUCE
3 tablespoons sliced almonds
One 12-ounce jar roasted red peppers, drained
2 tablespoons avocado or sunflower oil
1 tablespoon fresh lemon juice
1 garlic clove, minced
¼ teaspoon kosher salt
2 teaspoons chopped fresh parsley

FOR THE BROCCOLINI
1½ pounds broccolini, trimmed
1 tablespoon kosher salt
1 tablespoon sliced almonds

1. To prepare the sauce: Preheat the oven to 325°F. Spread the almonds for the sauce and the broccolini on a rimmed baking sheet. Roast for 8 minutes, or until lightly browned and fragrant. Set aside 1 tablespoon of toasted almond to garnish the broccolini.

2. Add all the ingredients for the sauce except for the parsley to the bowl of a food processor fitted with the S blade and blend until well combined. Then add the parsley and pulse a few times. Taste for seasoning. This sauce will last for up to a week stored in an airtight container or jar in the refrigerator.

3. Next, prepare the broccolini. In a large stockpot, bring 4 to 5 quarts of water to a boil and add the salt.

4. Set up a large bowl with ice water and set aside.

5. Once the water is boiling, drop in the broccolini and cook for about 2 minutes, or until the broccolini is just tender. Using metal tongs, immediately transfer the broccolini to the ice water, stopping the cooking process.

6. Drain the broccolini and place on a paper towel–lined plate to drain the excess water.

7. To serve, spoon and smooth the roasted red pepper sauce onto a serving plate. Top the sauce with the broccolini and garnish with sliced almonds over the top.

NOTES:

- You can substitute chopped walnuts, cashews, or pinenuts for the almonds.
- Feel free to substitute broccoli or green beans for the broccolini if you have trouble finding it.

FRESH UDON NOODLES
with Creamy Peanut Sauce

Udon noodles are known for their thick and slightly chewy texture, as well as their unique ability to absorb flavors, making them an ideal foundation for cold noodle dishes. In this beloved Feast & Fettle dish, they're tossed in a creamy peanut sauce that skillfully balances sweet, savory, and citrusy notes. A bit of sriracha heat, spicy fresh ginger, and robust garlic amplifies the sauce, while the crunch of red cabbage, carrots, and bell pepper makes every bite a visual and flavorful delight.

SERVES 4

PREP TIME: **20 minutes**
COOKING TIME: **5 minutes**
TOTAL TIME: **about 25 minutes**

FOR THE SAUCE
¼ cup smooth peanut butter
2 tablespoons honey
2 tablespoons fresh orange juice
1 tablespoon low-sodium soy sauce (or tamari)
1 tablespoon fresh lime juice
1 tablespoon sesame oil
1 teaspoon fresh ginger, peeled and minced
1 teaspoon sriracha sauce
1 garlic clove, minced
½ teaspoon kosher salt, more if needed

FOR THE NOODLES
1 pound fresh udon noodles
½ cup shredded carrots
½ cup seeded and thinly sliced red bell pepper
⅓ cup thinly sliced red cabbage
¼ cup frozen edamame, thawed
2 teaspoons toasted sesame seeds
2 tablespoons thinly sliced scallions

1 To make the sauce: Add all the ingredients to the bowl of a food processor fitted with the S blade and blend until smooth. Taste for seasoning. This sauce will last for up to a week stored in an airtight container or jar in the refrigerator.

2 To prepare the noodles: Bring 4 to 5 quarts of water to a boil. Add the noodles and cook for 3 to 4 minutes, or until tender but not overcooked. Drain and rinse the noodles under cold running water to stop the cooking process. Allow to drain for a few minutes before transferring the noodles to a large mixing bowl.

3 Add the carrots, peppers, cabbage, and edamame to the noodles along with the peanut sauce and toss well to combine. Taste for seasoning.

4 To serve, transfer the noodles to a large serving bowl and garnish with the toasted sesame seeds and the scallions.

NOTE:

If you have trouble finding fresh udon noodles, you can substitute dried udon noodles. Just follow the package instructions for cooking time.

TAGLIATELLE

with Slow-Roasted Tomatoes & Basil Cream Sauce

For those evenings when you crave a gourmet experience at home, a fresh pasta dish like this one truly hits the mark. Fresh tagliatelle stands out with its distinct tenderness and quick cooking time, especially when compared to its dried counterpart. The sauce is a rich combination of reduced heavy cream and butter, finished with freshly grated Parmesan cheese and fragrant basil. Now, let's talk about the slow-roasted tomatoes. While they do demand a bit more patience, clocking in over an hour of oven time, I can assure you the concentrated tomato flavor they bring is an absolute game changer. An added protein is not necessary, but consider topping with pan-seared shrimp or thinly sliced grilled chicken breast. This dish pairs wonderfully with the Kale & Cabbage Caesar Salad (page 75).

SERVES 4

PREP TIME: **10 minutes**
COOKING TIME: **1 hour 20 minutes**
TOTAL TIME: **1 hour 30 minutes**

2 cups cherry tomatoes, halved lengthwise

1 tablespoon extra virgin olive oil

4½ teaspoons kosher salt, more if needed

¼ teaspoon freshly cracked black pepper, more if needed

1½ cups heavy cream

2 tablespoons unsalted butter

¼ teaspoon dried basil

2 garlic cloves, minced

⅓ cup freshly grated Parmesan cheese

1 tablespoon fresh basil, roughly chopped, plus more for garnish

1 pound fresh tagliatelle pasta

1   Adjust the oven rack to the middle position and heat to 275°F.

2   Add the cherry tomatoes, olive oil, 1 teaspoon of the salt, and pepper to a bowl and toss to combine. Place the cherry tomatoes cut side up on a rimmed baking sheet.

3   Roast for 80 to 90 minutes, or until the edges are dried but the center is still a bit juicy. Set aside to cool.

4   Bring 4 to 5 quarts of water and 1 tablespoon of the salt to a boil in a large pot. While the water is boiling, start to prepare the sauce.

5   Add the heavy cream and butter to a large skillet over medium heat, bring to a simmer, and allow to thicken for 5 to 8 minutes.

6   Whisk in the basil, ½ teaspoon of the salt, garlic, and Parmesan cheese. Turn off the heat and stir in the fresh basil. Taste for seasoning.

7   Once the water starts boiling, add the tagliatelle and cook for 2 to 3 minutes, or until al dente. Drain and immediately add to the basil cream sauce, tossing to combine.

8   To serve, transfer the tagliatelle to a large serving platter, topping with the roasted cherry tomatoes and freshly chopped basil.

NOTE:

You can substitute dried tagliatelle for fresh tagliatelle; follow the package instructions for cooking time.

GRILLED FLANK STEAK

with Sweet Basil Chimichurri Sauce

Chimichurri, a popular herbal sauce from Argentina, traditionally uses parsley as the foundation. However, Feast & Fettle's iteration offers a fun twist. Aromatic fresh basil is paired with fresh garlic and crushed red pepper flakes for a bit of a kick. Brightened by red wine vinegar, this sauce impeccably complements the robust beefiness of the flank steak.

SERVES 4 OR 5

PREP TIME: **10 minutes**
COOKING TIME: **10 minutes**
TOTAL TIME: **about 20 minutes, plus cooling time**

FOR THE SAUCE
1 cup fresh parsley leaves, roughly chopped
½ cup fresh basil leaves, roughly chopped
½ cup avocado or sunflower oil
2 tablespoons red wine vinegar
1 tablespoon fresh lemon juice
2 garlic cloves, minced
½ teaspoon granulated sugar
½ teaspoon kosher salt, more if needed
½ teaspoon dry oregano
¼ teaspoon crushed red pepper flakes

FOR THE STEAK
1½ to 2 pounds flank steak, trimmed of excess silver skin, keep some fat
1 teaspoon avocado or sunflower oil
1 to 2 teaspoons kosher salt
¼ teaspoon freshly cracked black pepper, more if needed

1 To make the sauce: Add the parsley and basil to the bowl of a food processor fitted with the S blade. Pulse a few times.

2 Add the remaining ingredients and pulse until just combined. Taste for seasoning. This sauce will last for up to a week stored in an airtight container or jar in the refrigerator.

3 Now prepare the steak. Allow the grill to preheat on high for about 10 minutes. Clean and oil the grilling grates.

4 While the grill is heating, rub the oil over the steak and season both sides with salt and pepper.

5 Grill the steak until well marked on both sides, cooking for about 4 minutes per side, or until the internal temperature reaches 125° to 135°F for medium-rare on an instant-read thermometer.

6 Transfer the steak to a large cutting board and allow to rest for 10 minutes before slicing against the grain.

7 To serve, arrange slices of steak on a large serving plate and drizzle with the chimichurri sauce.

NOTE:

You can substitute skirt steak or flat iron steak for the flank steak in this recipe.

BROWN SUGAR MUSTARD-GLAZED HOLIDAY HAM

This one is a real stunner! Born out of Feast & Fettle's special Christmas and Easter menus, this recipe is surprisingly straightforward for any home cook. We use bone-in, spiral-sliced ham—a fully cooked ham that is artfully presliced using a special machine. Once gently warmed, we crank up the heat and lavishly brush the ham all over with a sticky sweet yet tangy glaze. Think of this glaze as a sauce that coats and caramelizes, giving the ham a lustrous shine, succulent flavor, and those irresistibly crispy edges.

SERVES 8 TO 10

PREP TIME: **35 minutes** (this includes bringing the ham up to room temperature)
COOKING TIME: **1 hour 40 minutes**
TOTAL TIME: **2 hours 15 minutes**

FOR THE GLAZE
⅓ **cup brown sugar**
3 tablespoons whole-grain mustard
2 tablespoons Dijon mustard
2 tablespoons apple cider vinegar
2 tablespoons avocado or sunflower oil
½ **teaspoon kosher salt**
¼ **teaspoon ground cinnamon**
¼ **teaspoon ground cloves** (optional)

FOR THE HAM
One 6- to 7-pound spiral-sliced, bone-in ham

1   To make the glaze: Add all the ingredients to a saucepan over medium heat and whisk until the sugar completely dissolves, about 3 minutes. Remove from the heat and set aside to cool.

2   Next, take the ham out of the refrigerator and let it sit at room temperature for 30 minutes to an hour; this will allow the ham to cook more evenly.

3   Adjust the oven rack to the lower position and heat to 300°F.

4   Wrap the ham tightly in aluminum foil and place on a rimmed baking sheet. Transfer to the oven and cook for 80 to 95 minutes, or until the internal temperature reaches 125°F to 130°F on an instant-read thermometer. Remove from the oven and unwrap the ham, draining any liquid that has accumulated on the baking sheet.

5   Increase the oven temperature to 425°F. Brush the ham all over with about one-third of the glaze and bake for 10 minutes. Remove the ham from the oven and brush with another one-third of the glaze and bake for another 8 to 10 minutes, or until the outside is crispy and deeply browned. Remove from the oven and brush all over with the remaining glaze and let rest for about 10 minutes before slicing and serving.

ROASTED RACK OF LAMB
with Cherry Port Sauce

Preparing a rack of lamb at home might sound like a tall order, but it's easier than you might think. Using an instant-read thermometer ensures that sought-after medium-rare finish. However, it's the cherry port sauce that truly steals the show. Its sweetness, from the frozen cherries and fruity port wine, is beautifully offset by the tangy balsamic vinegar, which effortlessly balances the dish's overall richness. This dish is a surefire winner when you're aiming to impress.

SERVES 4 TO 6

PREP TIME: **10 minutes**
COOKING TIME: **35 minutes**
TOTAL TIME: **about 45 minutes, plus resting time**

FOR THE SAUCE
½ cup ruby port wine
½ cup red cherries, frozen
2 tablespoons balsamic vinegar
1 tablespoon maple syrup
½ teaspoon kosher salt
1 tablespoon unsalted butter

FOR THE LAMB
2 racks of lamb, 8 ribs per rack
1 teaspoon kosher salt
¼ to ½ teaspoon freshly cracked black pepper
2 tablespoons avocado or sunflower oil
1 tablespoon Dijon mustard
1 tablespoon Classic Mayonnaise (page 42) or store-bought
⅓ cup fresh parsley, finely chopped
3 teaspoons fresh thyme, finely chopped

1 To prepare the sauce: Add the wine, cherries, balsamic vinegar, maple syrup, and salt to a saucepan over medium-high heat and bring to a boil. Let the mixture reduce for 8 to 10 minutes. Turn off the heat and whisk in the butter.

2 Transfer the mixture to a high-speed blender and blend until smooth. Alternatively, you can blend using a stick blender. This sauce will last for up to a week stored in an airtight container or jar in the refrigerator.

3 To prepare the lamb: Pat the racks dry with a paper towel. Season both sides with salt and pepper.

4 Add the oil to a large cast-iron or stainless steel skillet over medium-high heat. Place both racks (or one at a time if needed) in the skillet and sear fat side down for 3 minutes, or until golden brown. Using tongs, hold the racks upright to sear the bottom, for another 2 to 3 minutes. Transfer the racks to a rimmed baking sheet.

5 Adjust the oven rack to the top one-third of the oven and heat to 425°F.

6 In a small bowl, whisk together the Dijon mustard and mayonnaise and brush over the top of each rack. Combine the parsley and thyme and press into the mayonnaise mixture.

7 Roast for 20 to 25 minutes, or until the internal temperature in the center of the rack reaches 130° to 135°F on an instant-read thermometer. Let the racks rest for 5 to 10 minutes before slicing into chops and serving with the cherry port sauce.

NOTES:
- You can substitute Chianti or merlot for the port wine in the sauce.
- When carving the lamb racks, note that the ribs curve and don't align straight with the meat. To cut the ribs evenly, guide the knife closely along the curve of each bone.

HERB-CRUSTED PORK TENDERLOIN

with Fresh Cranberry Sauce

This aromatic blend of thyme, rosemary, and sage creates a delightful herbaceous crust on the pork tenderloin, which, when paired with fresh cranberry sauce, finds its savory flavors beautifully complemented by the cranberries' inherent tartness. Preparing fresh cranberry sauce at home is quick and easy, coming together with just six simple ingredients. The infusion of orange juice, fragrant orange peel, sugar, and cinnamon elevates the tartness of the cranberries and introduces a citrusy warmth to the sauce. So the next time you're tempted to reach for the store-bought cranberry sauce, consider this: With minimal effort, you can achieve a depth of flavor that's leagues beyond the canned variety.

SERVES 4 OR 5

PREP TIME: **10 minutes**
COOKING TIME: **25 minutes**
TOTAL TIME: **about 35 minutes, plus cooling time**

FOR THE SAUCE
One 12-ounce bag fresh cranberries
1 cup granulated sugar
½ cup fresh orange juice
½ cup water
2 thick slices orange peel
1 cinnamon stick

FOR THE PORK
2 tablespoons finely chopped fresh thyme
1 tablespoon finely chopped fresh rosemary
½ teaspoon ground sage (optional)
1 teaspoon kosher salt
¼ teaspoon ground black pepper
2 tablespoons avocado or sunflower oil
1¼ pounds pork tenderloin

1   To make the sauce: Add all the ingredients to a saucepan over medium-high heat and bring to boil, reduce the heat to a simmer, and cook for about 10 minutes.

2   Remove from the heat and let cool; the sauce will continue to thicken as it cools. This sauce will last for up to 2 weeks stored in an airtight container or jar in the refrigerator.

3   To make the pork: Adjust the oven rack to the middle position and preheat to 425°F.

4   In a small bowl, mix together the herbs, salt, and pepper until well combined. Rub the herb mixture all over the pork tenderloin.

5   Add the oil to a large cast-iron skillet or stainless steel pan over medium-high heat. Sear the pork tenderloin, for 2 to 3 minutes per side, or until nicely browned.

6   Transfer the pork to a rimmed baking sheet and place in the oven for 14 to 16 minutes, or until the pork reaches an internal temperature of 140°F in the center on an instant-read thermometer. Allow to rest for 10 minutes before slicing and serving with the cranberry sauce.

ROASTED SALMON
with Miso Teriyaki Sauce

The heart of this delectable dish is the sauce, a melding of umami-rich miso and soy sauce. The addition of brown sugar lends a sweet note and also helps achieve a beautifully charred exterior on the salmon. White miso is easily found at most grocery stores these days, due to its growing popularity as a versatile culinary ingredient. For a dinner full of flavor, pair this salmon with Sautéed Snap Peas with Kimchi-Miso Butter (page 113) and some steamed jasmine rice.

SERVES 4

PREP TIME: **5 minutes**
MARINATING TIME: **30 minutes**
COOKING TIME: **15 minutes**
TOTAL TIME: **about 50 minutes**

FOR THE SAUCE
½ cup low-sodium soy sauce (or tamari)
½ cup water
⅓ cup packed dark or light brown sugar
1 tablespoon white miso
1 tablespoon avocado or sunflower oil
1 teaspoon grated fresh ginger
1 garlic clove, grated

FOR THE SALMON
4 salmon fillets, 6 ounces each

1   To make the sauce: In a small saucepan, whisk together all the ingredients. Bring the mixture to a boil. Then reduce to a simmer and cook for 6 to 8 minutes, or until the sauce has slightly thickened.

2   Remove from the heat, pour into a bowl and place in the refrigerator, whisking occasionally to cool completely. This sauce will last for up to 2 weeks stored in an airtight container or jar in the refrigerator.

3   To prepare the salmon: Place it in a plastic zip-lock bag and add half of the miso teriyaki sauce, reserving the other half for a finishing sauce. Refrigerate and marinate the salmon in the sauce for at least 30 minutes or up to 24 hours.

4   Adjust the oven rack to the top one-third position and heat to 450°F.

5   Transfer the salmon to an aluminum foil–lined rimmed baking sheet and cook for 8 minutes. Then **broil** for another 6 to 8 minutes or until deeply browned on top and the center reaches an internal temperature of 130° to 135°F on an instant-read thermometer.

6   Serve immediately with a drizzle of the remaining miso teriyaki sauce over the top.

NOTE:

You can use salmon fillets with or without skin for this recipe.

SEARED CHICKEN THIGHS

with Mushroom-Garlic Gravy

Every bite of this dish is like a warm hug, perfect for those days when comfort food is paramount. The browning of the chicken doesn't just lend an appetizing hue, it also leaves behind flavorful browned bits that set the stage for a decadent gravy. Mushrooms and garlic sautéed to perfection in a fragrant medley of butter and fresh thyme, and the addition of sherry wine, give the gravy a subtle depth. A bit of heavy cream at the end introduces a luxurious richness. It's the gravy that makes the entire dish utterly irresistible, especially when spooned generously over a side of creamy mashed potatoes.

SERVES 4 OR 5

PREP TIME: **10 minutes**
COOKING TIME: **25 minutes**
TOTAL TIME: **about 35 minutes**

8 chicken thighs, boneless and skinless

2 to 3 teaspoons kosher salt

½ teaspoon ground black pepper

2 tablespoons avocado or sunflower oil

3 tablespoons unsalted butter

1 pound cremini or baby bella mushrooms, sliced

4 garlic cloves, minced

½ teaspoon dried thyme

¼ cup all-purpose flour

¼ cup sherry wine

2 cups low-sodium chicken stock (homemade or store-bought)

2 tablespoons heavy cream (optional)

1 tablespoon chopped fresh parsley

1 Lightly pat the chicken thighs dry with a paper towel and season both sides with salt and pepper.

2 Add the oil to a Dutch oven over medium-high heat and sear the chicken for about 3 minutes per side, or until nicely golden brown. Reduce the heat to medium and transfer the chicken to a plate.

3 Add the butter to the Dutch oven and, once melted, add the mushrooms and let cook for about 3 minutes.

4 Stir in the garlic, 1 teaspoon of the salt, ¼ teaspoon of the pepper, and thyme and cook for another 2 to 3 minutes before sprinkling the flour over the top of the mushroom mixture and cooking for another minute or so.

5 Deglaze the pan with the sherry wine, scraping up any browned bits from the bottom of the skillet and allowing the wine to reduce by half, before adding the chicken stock.

6 Bring the gravy to a simmer, nestle the chicken thighs into the gravy, and cover. Let cook for 6 to 8 minutes, or until the internal temperature of the chicken reaches 165°F on an instant-read thermometer. Stir in the heavy cream, if using, and garnish with the parsley.

NOTES:

- You can substitute thinly sliced chicken breast for the chicken thighs.
- You can substitute white button mushrooms for the cremini mushrooms.

WHOLE ROASTED RED SNAPPER
with Spicy Zhoug Sauce

Cooking a whole fish might feel daunting, but with a fishmonger handling the scaling and gutting, it's a straightforward endeavor with a stunning payoff. The red snapper's mildly sweet and firm flesh thrives under high-heat roasting. This fish has a subtle flavor, and the tangy and spicy kick of the Middle Eastern zhoug sauce adds just the zing it needs.

SERVES 2 OR 3

PREP TIME: **10 minutes**
COOKING TIME: **25 minutes**
TOTAL TIME: **about 35 minutes**

FOR THE SAUCE
1 jalapeño, roughly chopped

3 garlic cloves

1 cup fresh cilantro leaves, roughly chopped

½ teaspoon ground cumin

½ teaspoon ground coriander

½ teaspoon kosher salt, more if needed

2 tablespoons lime juice

½ cup avocado or sunflower oil

¼ teaspoon red chili flakes

FOR THE FISH
1 whole red snapper (2 to 2½ pounds, or 2 smaller red snapper), scaled and gutted

½ teaspoon kosher salt

1 tablespoon avocado or sunflower oil

½ small red onion, thinly sliced into rounds

1. To make the sauce: In the bowl of a food processor fitted with an S blade, add the jalapeños, garlic, cilantro, cumin, coriander, and salt. Pulse a few times.

2. With the food processor running, add the lime juice and oil, scraping down the sides until the sauce is mostly smooth. Stir in the chili flakes and taste for seasoning. Set aside. This sauce will last for up to a week stored in an airtight container or jar in the refrigerator.

3. To prepare the fish: Adjust the oven rack to the middle position and heat to 450°F. Line a rimmed baking sheet with parchment paper and set aside.

4. Make sure the fins are cut off the fish, leaving only the tail. Pat the fish dry with a paper towel, then using a sharp knife score both sides of the fish in two or three diagonal lines about 1 inch apart, cutting through the flesh down to the bone.

5. Season the skin and inside the cavity with the salt, then rub the fish all over with the oil. Stuff the cavity with the sliced onions and transfer to the baking sheet.

6. Roast for about 25 minutes, or until the internal temperature reaches 135°F on an instant-read thermometer and the fish easily flakes with a fork. Serve immediately.

7. To serve, place the fish on a large serving platter and liberally spoon the spicy zhoug sauce over the top.

NOTE:

You can substitute black sea bass or branzino for the red snapper.

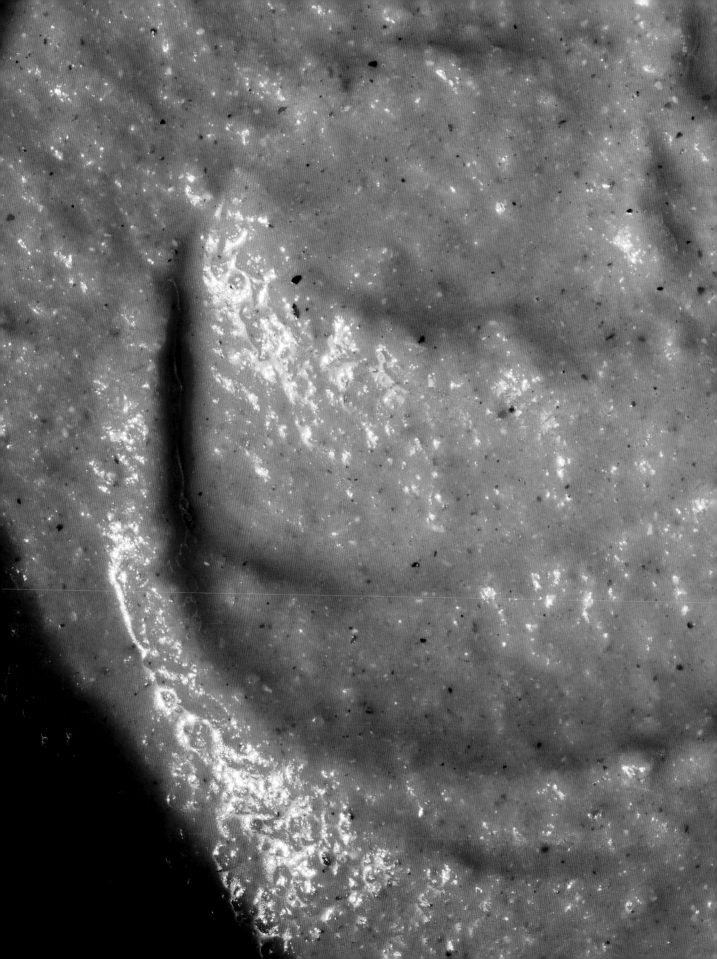

CHAPTER 7

SIMMER SAUCES

Unlike traditional sauces that accompany or garnish dishes, simmer sauces are deeply woven into the fabric of the meal itself. These sauces are part of the cooking process, allowing for an intense marriage of flavors. Braised Moroccan Chicken Tagine (page 159) is a perfect example of this technique. The succulent chicken thighs and tender vegetables braise together in a slightly sweet, deeply spiced Middle Eastern–inspired sauce.

Simmer sauces bring together a host of ingredients that collectively enrich the dish's flavor. One dish that exemplifies this is Chouriço & Pepper Shakshuka (page 163), where eggs are poached to perfection amid a robust tomato sauce with notes of fresh garlic, Portuguese chouriço, and sweet paprika.

Today, grocery store shelves are lined with an array of premade simmer sauces, which are irresistibly convenient for busy evenings. But the effort put into preparing your own sauce at home is definitely worth it: There's a unique charm and satisfaction in crafting a simmer sauce from scratch, tweaking flavors as you see fit. If you're short on time and need a flavorful dinner that can be ready in 30 minutes or less, consider Portobello Mushroom Lomo Saltado (page 150) or Steamed Mussels with Spicy Harissa Broth (page 164). If you have time for a more involved recipe, try Salsa Verde Braised Chicken (page 160).

PORTOBELLO MUSHROOM LOMO SALTADO

We are always looking for unique and flavorful vegetarian entrées at Feast & Fettle, and this dish is our vegetarian spin on a traditional Peruvian classic: lomo saltado. More than a mere stir-fry, this dish harmoniously marries distinct ingredients. The sauce, a blend of soy sauce, red wine vinegar, cumin, and fresh garlic, plays a pivotal role in seasoning the entire dish. Traditionally, lomo saltado is always served with french fries and occasionally white rice, which are the perfect companions to soak up every drop of the delectable sauce.

SERVES 4

PREP TIME: **10 minutes**
COOKING TIME: **15 minutes**
TOTAL TIME: about **25 minutes**

1 to 1½ pounds portobello mushroom caps

4 tablespoons avocado or sunflower oil

1 teaspoon kosher salt, more if needed

1 medium red onion, halved, cut into thick slices

2 ripe Roma tomatoes, sliced into wedges

3 to 4 garlic cloves, minced

½ teaspoon ground cumin

1 tablespoon red wine vinegar

1½ tablespoons soy sauce or tamari

½ teaspoon cornstarch

2 tablespoons chopped cilantro leaves

1   Gently twist off the stems of the mushrooms and wipe them down with a damp paper towel or rinse quickly under cold water. Use a spoon to gently scrape out the gills and discard. Slice the mushrooms into ¾- to 1-inch-thick slices.

2   Add 2 tablespoons of oil to a large skillet or wok over medium-high heat, then add the mushrooms and cook, stirring frequently until they have released their juices and start to brown and caramelize, 5 to 6 minutes, then season with salt. Transfer the mushrooms to a plate and set aside.

3   Add the remaining 2 tablespoons of oil to a large skillet or wok over medium-high heat, then add the red onions and cook until tender and slightly translucent, 6 to 8 minutes. Add the tomatoes, garlic, and cumin and allow to cook for another few minutes, or until the tomato starts to break down a bit.

4   Add the vinegar, soy sauce, and cornstarch to the vegetable mixture. Once it starts bubbling, reduce the heat to low and let simmer for 1 to 2 minutes. Add the portobello mushrooms to the vegetable mixture and gently stir to combine. Taste for seasoning.

5   Transfer to a large shallow serving bowl and garnish with cilantro.

NOTES:

- I always recommend removing the gills of portobello mushroom caps, as they can sometimes trap dirt or sand.
- This recipe is traditionally made with steak; if portobello mushrooms aren't your thing, substitute skirt steak or flank steak for the mushrooms.

VEGETABLE THAI GREEN CURRY

Packed with a vibrant array of vegetables, every bite of this dish is bursting with fresh flavors and delightful textures, largely thanks to the fragrant Thai green curry paste. Rich coconut milk and a touch of brown sugar balance out the sauce's spiciness. Thai basil imparts a subtle anise undertone and makes the curry a bit more aromatic. This curry is substantial on its own when served over steamed jasmine rice, but feel free to add seared tofu or shrimp for your protein needs.

SERVES 4

PREP TIME: **20 minutes**
COOKING TIME: **15 minutes**
TOTAL TIME: **about 35 minutes**

2 tablespoons avocado or sunflower oil

2 garlic cloves, minced

2 teaspoons minced fresh ginger

3 to 4 tablespoons Thai green curry paste (Maesri or Thai Kitchen)

One 14-ounce can full-fat coconut milk

½ cup water

2 to 3 teaspoons coconut sugar or brown sugar

½ teaspoon kosher salt, plus more to taste

2 medium carrots, peeled and sliced, ¼ inch on a diagonal

½ medium yellow onion, thickly sliced

1 medium summer squash, diced large

1 medium red bell pepper, seeded, diced large

1 cup packed snow peas, trimmed

One 8-ounce can water chestnuts, drained

¼ cup packed Thai basil leaves

1 tablespoon fresh lime juice

1 Add the oil to a large skillet or saucepan over medium heat. Add the garlic, ginger, and curry paste and cook until fragrant, about 2 minutes. Whisk in the coconut milk, water, coconut sugar, and salt and bring to a simmer. Taste for seasoning.

2 Add the carrots and onion to the curry mixture and let cook for 5 to 8 minutes before adding the summer squash and bell peppers, cooking for another 5 minutes, or until the vegetables are tender. Add the snow peas and cook for 30 seconds before adding the water chestnuts, Thai basil, and lime juice. Remove from the heat and serve over steamed rice.

NOTES:

- You can find Thai green curry paste at your local Asian market or in the Asian section at most grocery stores. Keep in mind that heat profiles can vary significantly from brand to brand.

- You can find Thai basil at your local Asian market; if you have trouble finding it, you can use regular fresh basil, but the curry will have a slightly different flavor profile.

- Feel free to substitute Japanese eggplant, broccoli, zucchini, or green beans for the vegetables listed in this recipe.

TOFU TIKKA MASALA

Here's a vegetarian take on chicken tikka masala. This dish starts with a warm and aromatic blend of spices, highlighted by sweet paprika and garam masala, which create a foundation for the luscious tomato-based sauce. Infused with undertones of fresh garlic and ginger, the sauce deepens in complexity as it simmers. A splash of heavy cream, a squeeze of lemon juice, and a sprinkle of fresh cilantro brings the flavors together. For the perfect pairing, serve it with a warm piece of naan, ideal for soaking up every drop of the rich, flavorful sauce.

SERVES 4

PREP TIME: **10 minutes**
COOKING TIME: **25 minutes**
TOTAL TIME: **about 35 minutes**

1 tablespoon sweet paprika

2 teaspoons garam masala

1 teaspoon ground cumin

1 teaspoon ground coriander

½ teaspoon ground turmeric

¼ teaspoon cayenne pepper, more if needed

½ teaspoon granulated sugar

2 teaspoons kosher salt, more if needed

½ teaspoon ground black pepper

2 tablespoons avocado or sunflower oil

3 garlic cloves, minced or grated

2 teaspoons minced or grated fresh ginger

One 28-ounce can whole peeled tomatoes, crushed by hand

2 tablespoons heavy cream

2 tablespoons chopped fresh cilantro

1 to 2 tablespoons fresh lemon juice

One 16-ounce block super firm tofu, cut into ½- to 1-inch cubes

1 In a small bowl, whisk together the paprika, garam masala, cumin, coriander, turmeric, cayenne pepper, sugar, salt, and pepper.

2 Add the oil to a large skillet or Dutch oven over medium-high heat, then add the garlic and ginger and cook for about 1 minute, before adding the spices and cooking until fragrant, another 1 to 2 minutes.

3 Add the tomatoes to the spice mixture. Bring to a simmer and let it cook for about 10 minutes. Using an immersion blender or high-speed blender, blend the masala sauce until smooth. Stir in the heavy cream, cilantro, and lemon juice. Taste for seasoning.

4 Add the tofu to the masala sauce and continue to simmer for another 8 to 10 minutes. Serve over steamed rice or with warm naan.

NOTES:

• If you have trouble finding super firm tofu, you can substitute extra firm tofu. Make sure to press extra firm tofu for 20 to 30 minutes before using in the recipe.

• You can substitute chickpeas or paneer for the tofu for an alternative vegetarian protein option.

CHEESY PULLED CHICKEN ENCHILADAS

This enchilada recipe is set to become your weeknight hero meal, loved by the whole family and easily assembled when you prep the components ahead of time. While opting for store-bought rotisserie chicken is an absolute game changer, the real MVP of this dish is the homemade red enchilada sauce. Preparing it from scratch brings depth and authenticity to the enchiladas, something many store-bought varieties can't match. A pro tip: Whip up this flavorful sauce beforehand and stash it away for making a quick, flavor-packed meal when you need it.

SERVES 4 OR 5

PREP TIME: **20 minutes**
COOKING TIME: **40 minutes**
TOTAL TIME: **1 hour 10 minutes**

FOR THE SAUCE
2 tablespoons avocado or sunflower oil
1 small yellow onion, diced
2 tablespoons chili powder
1 teaspoon ground cumin
½ teaspoon granulated garlic
½ teaspoon onion powder
1 teaspoon kosher salt, more to taste
¼ teaspoon ground black pepper
1 tablespoon tomato paste
One 15-ounce can tomato sauce
One 4-ounce can diced green chilies
½ cup water, more if needed
1 teaspoon white vinegar

FOR THE ENCHILADAS
3 to 4 tablespoons avocado or sunflower oil, more if needed
Ten 6-inch corn tortillas
One 2- to 3-pound rotisserie chicken
1 cup corn, fresh or frozen
3 cups shredded Monterey Jack cheese
¼ cup fresh cilantro, chopped, plus more for garnish

1   To make the enchilada sauce: Heat the oil in a medium saucepan over medium-high heat. Add the onion and cook for about 5 minutes, or until the onion is translucent.

2   Add the chili powder, cumin, granulated garlic, onion powder, salt, and pepper and cook for about 1 minute. Add the tomato paste and cook for another minute or so. Pour in the tomato sauce, chilies, water, and vinegar and bring to a boil. Reduce to a simmer and cook for about 10 minutes.

3   Using an immersion blender or high-speed blender, blend the sauce until smooth, adding a bit more water if the mixture seems too thick. Taste for seasoning and adjust as needed. Set aside. This sauce will last for up to a week stored in an airtight container or jar in the refrigerator.

4   To prepare the enchiladas: Adjust the oven rack to the middle position and heat to 400°F. Spread about 1 cup of the enchilada sauce in the bottom of a 9-by-13-inch baking dish.

5   Heat the oil in a large skillet over medium heat. Using tongs, fry the corn tortillas one at a time in the oil for no longer than 15 seconds per side, adding more oil if needed. The tortillas should be soft not crispy. Transfer them to a paper towel–lined plate to drain. Cover with a damp paper towel while frying the remaining tortillas, ensuring they do not dry out.

6   Shred the meat from the rotisserie chicken and place in a mixing bowl with the corn, half of the cheese, cilantro, and about ½ cup of enchilada sauce. Toss to combine.

7 To assemble: Spoon the chicken mixture, about ½ cup, on top of the tortillas, one at a time. Roll the tortilla around the filling and place the enchilada seam side down in the prepared baking dish. Top with the remaining enchilada sauce, spreading it all over the top of the tortillas, and sprinkle with the remaining cheese.

8 Bake for 15 to 20 minutes, or until the cheese is melted and starting to lightly brown.

NOTES:

- Although using a rotisserie chicken is the quickest way to get flavorful shredded chicken, you could make the chicken at home: Bring water plus a bay leaf to a boil in a medium saucepan, adding 4 boneless, skinless chicken breasts (7 to 8 ounces each). Then immediately turn off the heat and let the chicken poach for 25 to 30 minutes. Allow to cool slightly before shredding.

- If you don't want to fry the tortillas, which helps to prevent the enchiladas from becoming soggy, you can wrap the tortillas in aluminum foil and place them in a 400°F oven for 10 to 15 minutes, or until they are heated through.

BRAISED MOROCCAN CHICKEN TAGINE

This dish just screams comfort food to me. Anything braised reminds me of relaxing weekend cooking when there's time to let a dish become something truly spectacular. This is a Northern African, specifically Moroccan, slow-cooked stew. It is named after the ceramic vessel it is traditionally prepared in, which is called a tagine. The star of this dish is the slightly sweet and spiced simmer sauce. During the braising process, the chicken thighs and vegetables tenderize and soak up all those delicious flavors. The addition of olives, lemon juice, and an abundance of fresh herbs at the end of the cooking process adds a dimension of brightness that balances out the sweetness of the sauce.

SERVES 4

PREP TIME: **15 minutes**
COOKING TIME: **1 hour 15 minutes**
TOTAL TIME: **1 hour 30 minutes**

2 pounds chicken thighs, boneless and skinless
3 teaspoons kosher salt
4 tablespoons extra virgin olive oil
1 teaspoon sweet paprika
1 teaspoon ground cumin
½ teaspoon ground ginger
¼ teaspoon ground coriander
¼ teaspoon ground cinnamon
¼ teaspoon ground turmeric
½ cup diced onion
3 medium carrots, peeled and diced
3 garlic cloves, minced
2 cups chicken stock, homemade or low-sodium store-bought
1 bay leaf
1 tablespoon apricot jam or honey
1 teaspoon lemon zest
10 to 12 pitted Castelvetrano olives
½ cup fresh cilantro, chopped
¼ cup fresh parsley, chopped
1 tablespoon fresh lemon juice

1   Adjust the oven rack to the middle position and heat to 325°F.

2   Pat the chicken thighs dry with paper towels and season all over with half of the salt.

3   Add half of the olive oil to a Dutch oven over medium-high heat. Sear the chicken thighs on both sides until lightly golden brown, about 5 minutes per side. Turn off the heat and transfer the chicken to a plate; set aside.

4   In a small mixing bowl, make the spice blend: Add the remaining salt, paprika, cumin, ginger, coriander, cinnamon, and turmeric. Whisk together to combine and set aside.

5   Heat the Dutch oven over medium-high heat, adding the additional olive oil if needed, and sauté the onion and carrots until the onions are tender and translucent, 8 to 10 minutes. Add the garlic and cook for another minute or so.

6   Add the spice blend to the vegetable mixture and cook for another minute, or until the spices are fragrant.

7   Add the chicken stock, bay leaf, apricot jam, and lemon zest and bring to a boil. Add the chicken thighs back to the Dutch oven, cover, and turn off the heat.

8   Place the Dutch oven in the oven and braise for 55 to 60 minutes, or until the chicken is very tender.

9   Remove from the oven and stir in the olives, cilantro, parsley, and lemon juice. Shred the chicken with two forks and taste for seasoning.

SALSA VERDE BRAISED CHICKEN

Salsa verde, or "green sauce," showcases the uniquely acidic and almost citrusy essence of tomatillos. While they resemble small, unripe green tomatoes with a papery husk, their name, "little tomato," is a bit misleading as they belong to a class of their own. The deep flavor of the sauce emerges from the charred tomatillos, onions, and peppers. A touch of sugar balances the char of the vegetables, while fresh cilantro completes the taste profile. Braising chicken legs in this vibrant salsa mixture ensures they absorb the full range of flavors, while also yielding a delicious sauce that's perfect for drizzling.

SERVES 4

PREP TIME: **15 minutes**
COOKING TIME: **1 hour 15 minutes**
TOTAL TIME: **1 hour 30 minutes**

FOR THE SALSA
6 medium tomatillos
1 small white onion, peeled and quartered
2 poblano peppers, halved and seeded
1 jalapeño, halved (seeded for less spice)
1 to 2 tablespoons fresh lime juice
1 teaspoon kosher salt
½ teaspoon granulated sugar
¼ cup fresh cilantro, chopped

FOR THE CHICKEN
4 whole chicken legs, drumsticks and thighs, patted dry
1 teaspoon kosher salt
¼ teaspoon ground black pepper
2 tablespoons avocado or sunflower oil

1   To make the salsa: Adjust the oven rack to the highest setting and set to broil on high. Line a rimmed baking sheet with aluminum foil.

2   Remove the husks from the tomatillos and rinse well to remove the sticky residue. Dry and place on the prepared baking sheet with the onion, poblano peppers, and jalapeño pepper.

3   Broil for 6 to 8 minutes, or until the tomatillos are slightly charred on top and tender.

4   To a high-speed blender or food processor, add the roasted vegetables, lime juice, salt, sugar, and cilantro. Blend until combined, adding water if the salsa is too thick. Taste for seasoning and set aside. This salsa will last for up to a week stored in an airtight container or jar in the refrigerator.

5   To prepare the chicken: Adjust the oven rack to the lower middle position and preheat to 350°F.

6   Dry the chicken legs with a paper towel and season all over with salt and pepper.

7   Add the oil to a Dutch oven over medium-high heat. Once the oil starts to shimmer, add the chicken legs skin side down, allowing them to brown for about 5 minutes before flipping and browning the other side for another 5 minutes. Transfer the chicken legs to a plate and set aside.

8   Pour the salsa verde into the Dutch oven and cook over medium heat, stirring occasionally, for about 5 minutes.

9   Place the chicken legs in the Dutch oven with the salsa verde and cover. Braise in the oven for 40 minutes, then remove the lid and cook for another 10 minutes, or until the chicken is tender and nicely browned. Serve chicken along with the salsa verde sauce.

CHOURIÇO & PEPPER SHAKSHUKA

When I first tasted shakshuka, with its gently poached eggs nestled in a spiced tomato and bell pepper sauce, I was instantly reminded of the comforting flavors of Portuguese chouriço and peppers. In my recipe, I merge these flavors, creating a sauce infused with onion, green bell pepper, and heavily seasoned chouriço, which delivers notes of paprika, chili, and garlic in every bite. The highlight of this dish? Breaking into those soft-poached eggs with a piece of crusty bread, and allowing it to soak up all the flavors from the sauce for that perfect bite.

SERVES 4 OR 5

PREP TIME: **10 minutes**
COOK TIME: **25 minutes**
TOTAL TIME: **about 35 minutes**

2 tablespoons extra virgin olive oil

1 medium onion, halved, thinly sliced

1 medium green bell pepper, seeded, thinly sliced

½ pound ground Portuguese chouriço

2 garlic cloves, sliced

1 teaspoon sweet paprika

One 28-ounce can whole peeled tomatoes, crushed by hand

1½ teaspoons kosher salt, plus more to taste

¼ teaspoon cracked black pepper

4 or 5 large eggs

1 or 2 tablespoons roughly chopped fresh cilantro

1 loaf crusty bread, sliced

1 Add the oil to a large skillet or cast-iron pan over medium heat. Add the onions and bell peppers and cook, while stirring, until soft, which should take 5 to 6 minutes.

2 Add the chouriço to the vegetable mixture and cook, stirring, for about 5 minutes. Add the garlic and paprika and cook until fragrant, about 30 seconds.

3 Pour in the tomatoes and season with the salt and black pepper. Lightly simmer until thickened, about 8 minutes.

4 Using a large spoon, create a slight well in the thickened sauce and break one egg directly into it. Repeat this process with the remaining eggs. Season each of the eggs with a pinch of kosher salt and cover the pan, cooking for 6 to 8 minutes, or until the egg whites are just set and the yolks are still runny.

5 Turn off the heat and garnish with cilantro. Serve immediately with torn crusty bread.

NOTE:

You can substitute chouriço links for the ground chouriço; cut the links into ¼- to ½-inch cubes.

STEAMED MUSSELS

with Spicy Harissa Broth

What's the most important element of a mussel dish? The broth! In my kitchen, it's all about crafting a broth so irresistible that reaching for crusty bread or a spoon to savor every last drop becomes second nature. The sautéed onion, bell pepper, and garlic serve as the base. But it's the Portuguese chouriço coupled with the harissa paste that truly elevates the flavor profile. If you're new to harissa, think of it as a spiced chili pepper paste that adds both depth and a gentle kick. As the mussels steam, they generously release their natural juices, lending a natural salinity to the broth. A splash of heavy cream thickens the broth and introduces a velvety richness, and a sprinkle of fresh cilantro adds an instant burst of brightness.

SERVES 3 OR 4

PREP TIME: **15 minutes**
COOK TIME: **15 minutes**
TOTAL TIME: **about 30 minutes**

2 to 3 pounds farm-raised mussels

2 tablespoons extra virgin olive oil

1 small yellow onion, halved, thinly sliced

1 medium red bell pepper, seeded, thinly sliced

4 garlic cloves, minced

½ pound ground Portuguese chouriço

1½ to 2 teaspoons harissa paste

¼ teaspoon kosher salt, plus more to taste

¾ cup white wine

3 tablespoons heavy cream

2 tablespoons roughly chopped fresh cilantro, plus more for garnish

1   Place the mussels in a colander in the sink and run them under cold water. Toss out any mussels with cracked shells or ones that are open and do not close when gently squeezed.

2   Scrub the outside shells to get rid of any visible debris and check for beards, the hairy growth where mussels attach themselves to objects. Using a dry paper towel, grasp it and pull firmly until it comes out. Place the cleaned mussels in a bowl and set aside.

3   Pour the oil into a stockpot or Dutch oven over medium heat. Add the onions and bell peppers and cook, stirring frequently, until the onions begin to soften and turn translucent, 5 to 6 minutes.

4   Add the garlic and chouriço and cook, stirring for another 5 minutes. Stir in the harissa paste and salt, then add the wine and bring to a gentle boil.

5   Add the cleaned mussels and cover, allowing the mussels to steam and open, about 5 minutes. Pour the heavy cream over the opened mussels, sprinkle the cilantro, and gently stir.

6   Transfer the mussels to serving bowls and garnish with additional cilantro. Serve immediately.

NOTES:

- I recommend farmed mussels because they are generally cleaner and easier to work with.

- Harissa pastes have varying spice levels. I suggest tasting the harissa paste and starting with the lesser amount and adding more if you would like more spice.

CHAPTER 8

SPICE BLENDS

Have you ever had that "aha!" moment when you realized the secret behind an unforgettable dish was just a pinch of a particular spice? It might be the touch of nutmeg added to a creamy roasted butternut squash soup or the sprinkle of smoked paprika over a roasted chicken. That's the magic of spices for me. With their potent flavors and aromatic qualities, they can effortlessly elevate a dish from "meh" to "mind-blowing."

Spices are derived from various parts of plants, including bark, flower buds, seeds, fruits, and roots. Each spice has its own unique flavor profile. Consider the vibrant golden turmeric, with its earthy potent flavor; or the sweet, woody taste of cinnamon. On the other hand, dried herbs come from the fragrant leaves of plants. They often provide more intense flavors compared to their fresh counterparts—bold, earthy dried oregano and sweet, pungent dried basil are but two examples.

Everyone has a favorite spice blend, whether it's everything bagel seasoning (see Everything Bagel Dinner Rolls, page 176) or za'atar seasoning (see Za'atar Roasted Sweet Potato Wedges, page 175). Spice blends create distinct and balanced flavor combinations comprised of a mix of spices, seeds, nuts, and often dried herbs. Making these blends at home allows you to customize flavors and ensures peak freshness. Although store-bought blends are convenient, they often lack the vibrancy of a freshly mixed combination.

Expired spices lack the potency and flavor of their fresh counterparts. Here are a few tips for sourcing fresh spices:

- Look for ones dated for freshness
- Purchase from brands known for small-batch production
- Choose spices at stores with a quick inventory turnover

Ground spices, while more subtle in flavor, integrate seamlessly into recipes and provide even distribution throughout. But for dishes that demand more vivid flavor, whole spices come into play. This chapter leans heavily on ground spices, primarily because they're readily available and simplify the cooking process. However, if you're comfortable with whole spices, feel free to use them freshly ground. A simple grind with a mortar and pestle or a quick whiz in a spice grinder will do the job, capturing the freshest flavor possible.

BABA GHANOUSH

with Egyptian Dukkah

The smoky, creamy essence of baba ghanoush is beautifully accented with a generous sprinkle of dukkah on top. The toasted hazelnuts and pine nuts are the soul of the dukkah, lending a buttery warmth and nicely complementing the cumin and coriander. A deep charring of the eggplants on the grill is key to achieving that signature smoky undertone. Blending slightly bitter tahini and a splash of fresh lemon juice transform the baba ghanoush into a delectable dip. This creamy, robust spread pairs perfectly with warm pita bread or naan.

SERVES 4 TO 6

PREP TIME: **10 minutes**
COOKING TIME: **35 minutes**
TOTAL TIME: **about 45 minutes, plus cooling and draining time**

FOR THE DUKKAH
(MAKES ABOUT ¾ CUP)
½ cup hazelnuts
2 tablespoons pine nuts
2 tablespoons toasted sesame seeds
1 teaspoon ground cumin
1 teaspoon ground coriander
½ teaspoon kosher salt
¼ teaspoon ground black pepper

FOR THE BABA GHANOUSH
2 pounds small to medium Italian
    eggplants
2 tablespoons fresh lemon juice
2 garlic cloves, grated
½ teaspoon kosher salt, more if
    needed
¼ cup tahini
¼ cup extra virgin olive oil, plus more
    as needed
2 tablespoons chopped fresh parsley
Pita bread, warmed

1   To make the dukkah: Adjust the oven rack to the middle position and preheat to 325°F.

2   Arrange the hazelnuts and pine nuts in a single layer on a rimmed baking sheet and roast for 8 to 10 minutes, or until the nuts are golden brown and fragrant.

3   Add the toasted nuts and the remaining dukkah ingredients to the bowl of a food processor fitted with the S blade and pulse until the nuts are coarsely chopped. Store the dukkah in an airtight container until ready to use.

4   To prepare the baba ghanoush: Allow the grill to preheat on medium-high for about 10 minutes. Clean and oil the grill grates.

5   Pierce the eggplants all over with a fork and place on the hot grill. Cook, turning frequently, for 20 to 25 minutes, or until the eggplants are charred all around and completely tender. Wrap the eggplants in foil and let rest for 10 minutes.

6   Cut the eggplants in half, place in a colander over a bowl, and allow most of the liquid to drain, about 15 minutes. Peel the charred skin and stem from the eggplant and discard along with the drained liquid.

7   Add the eggplant flesh to a mixing bowl and stir vigorously with a fork until it breaks down. Mix in the lemon juice, garlic, salt, and tahini until incorporated. While stirring, drizzle in the olive oil until the mixture achieves a creamy consistency. Stir in the parsley and taste for seasoning.

8   To serve, spread the baba ghanoush in a wide shallow bowl, sprinkle with the dukkah seasoning, and drizzle with a little extra olive oil. Serve with warm pita bread.

NOTE:

Instead of grilling, you can roast the eggplant, but it will not have the same smoky flavor as the grilled version. To roast, cut the eggplant in half lengthwise, score, and brush with olive oil. Place each half cut side down on a parchment-lined rimmed baking sheet and roast in a 425°F oven until the eggplant is completely tender, about 40 minutes.

CRISPY RANCH BAKED CAULIFLOWER

Cauliflower, on its own, might not be the most exciting vegetable on the block. But after roasting in a hot oven, it takes on an irresistible crispy texture. The homemade ranch-style seasoning—a blend of dried herbs and a duo of garlic and onion—coats each floret, ensuring every bite delivers a flavor-packed punch. This is an easy dish to prepare, and chances are you've got most of these seasonings hanging out in your pantry already.

SERVES 4

PREP TIME: **10 minutes**
COOKING TIME: **20 minutes**
TOTAL TIME: **about 30 minutes**

FOR RANCH SEASONING
(MAKES ABOUT ⅓ CUP)
1 tablespoon dried parsley
1 tablespoon granulated garlic
1 tablespoon onion powder
1 teaspoon dried dill
1 teaspoon dried chives (optional)
1 teaspoon kosher salt
½ teaspoon ground black pepper

FOR THE CAULIFLOWER
1 large head cauliflower, cut into florets
3 tablespoons avocado or sunflower oil
2 to 3 tablespoons ranch seasoning

1 To make the ranch seasoning: Whisk together all the ingredients in a mixing bowl. Store in an airtight container until ready to use.

2 To prepare the cauliflower: Adjust the oven rack to the middle position and preheat to 400°F. Line a rimmed baking sheet with parchment paper.

3 In a large mixing bowl, toss the cauliflower florets with the oil and ranch seasoning until well coated. Pour out onto the lined baking sheet and spread into an even layer.

4 Roast the cauliflower for 20 to 25 minutes, or until golden brown and crispy. Serve immediately.

ZA'ATAR ROASTED SWEET POTATO WEDGES

If you are unfamiliar with za'atar, it's a spice blend that's bursting with bright, slightly citrusy, herby, and toasty notes—a combination that effortlessly elevates the humble sweet potato. Traditional Middle Eastern za'atar is made with hyssop leaf, which is difficult to find in America. Thus, this blend calls up the familiar flavors of oregano and thyme, which lend a similar flavor profile. Roasting the sweet potato wedges accentuates their natural sweetness, creating a harmonious play between sweet and savory. These wedges pair beautifully with Whipped Feta Dip (page 54), a drizzle of olive oil, and a sprinkle of extra za'atar spice.

SERVES 4 TO 6

PREP TIME: **10 minutes**
COOKING TIME: **25 minutes**
TOTAL TIME: **about 35 minutes**

FOR THE ZA'ATAR SEASONING
(MAKES ABOUT ¼ CUP)
1 tablespoon dried thyme
1 tablespoon dried oregano
1 tablespoon sumac
1 tablespoon toasted sesame seeds
1 teaspoon kosher salt

FOR THE SWEET POTATOES
3 medium sweet potatoes, peeled and cut into equal-sized wedges
2 tablespoons extra virgin olive oil
1½ tablespoons za'atar seasoning

1 To make the za'atar seasoning: Whisk together all the ingredients in a mixing bowl. Store in an airtight container until ready to use.

2 To prepare the sweet potatoes: Adjust the oven rack to the center position and preheat to 400°F. Line a rimmed baking sheet with parchment paper.

3 In a large mixing bowl, toss together the sweet potato wedges, oil, and za'atar until well coated. Pour onto the parchment-lined baking sheet and spread out into an even layer.

4 Roast the sweet potatoes for about 15 minutes, then flip over and let them cook for another 10 to 15 minutes, or until crispy and golden brown. Serve immediately.

EVERYTHING BAGEL DINNER ROLLS

Diving in to homemade bread making might seem daunting, but this recipe offers a user-friendly technique for novices, with the help of instant yeast and a stand mixer. While these rolls are delightful in their simplicity, a sprinkle of homemade everything bagel seasoning elevates them to a gourmet treat. Preparing this iconic seasoning couldn't be simpler: Gather the ingredients, mix, and you're ready to sprinkle.

MAKES 15 ROLLS

PREP TIME: **15 minutes**
RISE TIME: **2 hours 30 minutes**
COOKING TIME: **25 minutes**
TOTAL TIME: **3 hours 10 minutes**

FOR THE EVERYTHING BAGEL
SEASONING (MAKES ABOUT
⅓ CUP)
1 tablespoon toasted sesame seeds
1 tablespoon black sesame seeds
2 teaspoons poppy seeds
2 teaspoons minced garlic
2 teaspoons minced onion
2 teaspoons Maldon Sea Salt Flakes

FOR THE ROLLS
½ cup (118 g) warm water (110°F)
2¼ teaspoons (1 packet) instant yeast
1 large egg
½ cup (120 g) warm whole milk
**6 tablespoons (85 g) unsalted butter,
     softened**
**3 tablespoons (38 g) granulated
     sugar**
1½ teaspoons (6 g) kosher salt
3½ (455 g) cups all-purpose flour

FOR THE TOPPING
1 large egg
1 tablespoon (15 g) whole milk
**2 to 3 tablespoons (16 to 24 g)
     everything bagel seasoning**

1   To make the seasoning: Whisk together all the ingredients in a mixing bowl and store in an airtight container until ready to use.

2   To prepare the rolls: Whisk together the warm water and yeast in the bowl of a stand mixer until combined. Then cover the bowl with a kitchen towel and let it sit for 5 minutes.

3   To the yeast mixture, add the egg, milk, butter, sugar, salt, and flour. Using the dough hook attachment, beat on low speed, then increase to medium and beat for 5 minutes until you have a soft, slightly sticky dough.

4   Transfer the dough to a lightly greased large mixing bowl and cover with plastic wrap or a clean kitchen towel. Let the dough rise in a warm spot for about 90 minutes, or until it doubles in size.

5   Lightly grease a 9-by-13-inch baking pan. Punch down the dough to deflate and divide into 15 pieces. Shape each piece into a round ball and place in the prepared pan. Cover the pan with lightly greased plastic wrap or a clean kitchen towel and let rise for 60 minutes, or until puffy.

6   Adjust the oven rack to the lower middle position and preheat to 350°F.

7   While you wait for the oven to preheat, you can prepare the egg wash. In a small bowl, whisk together the egg and milk. Then brush the egg wash over the tops of the rolls and sprinkle liberally with everything bagel seasoning. The egg and milk will help the seasoning stick to the rolls.

8 Bake the rolls for 20 to 25 minutes, or until golden brown on top. Remove from the oven and allow to cool slightly before turning them out of the pan and onto a cooling rack. Serve the rolls warm or at room temperature. Store the rolls, wrapped tightly in plastic wrap or in a plastic storage bag, at room temperature for up to 3 days.

NOTES:

- To avoid a dense dough, make sure to spoon and level your flour instead of scooping it directly out of the package. Or you can use the provided gram weight.
- Using a plastic dough scraper can be helpful for getting the dough out of the stand mixer bowl.

ROASTED BUTTERNUT SQUASH SOUP

with Spiced Pepitas

The inherent sweetness of butternut squash is unlocked through roasting, which also caramelizes its exterior. The result is a perfect base for this velvety soup. The blend of sweet cinnamon, spicy ginger, and fragrant nutmeg create a flavor infusion of spiced warmth. A generous pour of heavy cream, coupled with a drizzle of maple syrup, complements the squash's natural sweetness and lends a luscious mouthfeel. Candied pepitas, sweetened with brown sugar and echoing the soup's warming spice blend, introduce a delightful crunch and add a layer of flavor, making each spoonful a harmonious blend of creamy and crunchy.

SERVES 4

PREP TIME: **10 minutes**
COOKING TIME: **1 hour 20 minutes**
TOTAL TIME: **1 hour 30 minutes**

FOR THE SPICED PEPITAS
¼ cup packed brown sugar
1 tablespoon water
½ teaspoon ground cinnamon
¼ teaspoon ground ginger
⅛ teaspoon ground nutmeg
¼ teaspoon kosher salt
1 cup raw pepitas

FOR THE SOUP
1 medium butternut squash (2½ pounds), halved and seeded
1 tablespoon extra virgin olive oil
2 tablespoons unsalted butter
1 medium yellow onion, diced
2 garlic cloves, minced
½ teaspoon ground cinnamon
½ teaspoon ground ginger
¼ teaspoon ground nutmeg
1½ teaspoons kosher salt, more if needed
¼ teaspoon ground black pepper
2 tablespoons maple syrup
4 cups low-sodium vegetable stock
¼ cup heavy cream

1 To make the spiced pepitas: Line a rimmed quarter baking sheet with parchment paper.

2 Whisk together the brown sugar, water, and spices in a small saucepan over medium heat. Once the sugar dissolves and the mixture is bubbly, about 2 minutes, stir in the pepitas and cook for another minute or so.

3 Spread the pepitas out on the prepared baking sheet and cool for at least 20 minutes, or until fully dry, before breaking apart and storing in an airtight container until ready to use.

4 To make the soup: Adjust an oven rack to the middle position and preheat to 400°F. Line a rimmed baking sheet with parchment paper.

5 Place the butternut squash on the prepared baking sheet and brush with the oil. Flip the squash halves over so they are cut side down and roast for 50 to 60 minutes, or until the squash is very tender. Set aside to cool.

6 Once the squash has cooled enough to handle, scoop out the flesh and transfer to a mixing bowl, discarding the skins.

7 In a stockpot or large saucepan over medium-high heat, melt the butter. Add the onions and sauté until translucent, about 3 minutes. Stir in the garlic and cook for another minute, then add the cinnamon, ginger, nutmeg, salt, and pepper, and continue cooking for another minute.

8 Add the butternut squash flesh to the pot along with the maple syrup and vegetable stock and bring to boil. Reduce to a simmer and allow to cook for about 10 minutes. Blend the soup with an immersion blender until very smooth and stir in the heavy cream. Taste for seasoning.

NOTE:

You can substitute slivered almonds or chopped pecans for the pepitas.

GRILLED CHICKEN FAJITAS

Chicken fajitas venture into the zesty vibrant world of Tex-Mex cuisine, and what sets this dish apart is its interactive, family-style serving that allows everyone to personalize their fajita. The flavor backbone of these homemade fajitas is the spice blend: a medley of smoky chili powder, earthy warm cumin, and sweetly pungent paprika, all tied together with a touch of brown sugar that subtly balances the heat of the chili powder. Applied generously as a rub, this spice blend seasons the chicken with an intense, layered flavor profile. The sautéed bell peppers and onion, enlivened by a hint of jalapeño heat, provide a vibrant complement to the grilled chicken. When accompanied by warm flour tortillas and creamy avocado slices or Avocado Lime Crema (page 51), this dish celebrates shared moments around the table.

SERVES 4

PREP TIME: **15 minutes**
COOKING TIME: **18 minutes**
TOTAL TIME: **about 33 minutes**

FOR THE FAJITA SPICE
2 tablespoons chili powder
1 tablespoon sweet paprika
1 tablespoon ground cumin
1 tablespoon kosher salt
1 tablespoon granulated garlic
1 tablespoon brown sugar
1 teaspoon dried oregano
1 teaspoon onion powder
1 teaspoon ground black pepper

FOR THE FAJITAS
3 tablespoons avocado or sunflower oil
1 medium onion, ½ inch sliced
1 medium red bell pepper, ½ inch sliced
1 jalapeño pepper, seeded and thinly sliced
2 garlic cloves, thinly sliced
1½ pounds thin boneless, skinless chicken breasts
¼ cup plus 1 teaspoon fajita spice
8 flour tortillas, warmed
1 ripe avocado, sliced

1 To make the fajita spice mix: Whisk together all the ingredients in a mixing bowl. Store in an airtight container until ready to use.

2 To prepare the fajitas: Add 2 tablespoons of the oil to a large skillet over medium heat. Then add the onions and cook for about 3 minutes, before adding the bell peppers and jalapeño and cooking for another 3 minutes. Add the garlic and 1 teaspoon of the fajita spice and cook for another 30 seconds.

3 Allow the grill to preheat on high for about 10 minutes. Clean and oil the grill grates.

4 Place the chicken in a mixing bowl with the remaining 1 tablespoon oil and ¼ cup of fajita spice and, using your hands, rub the spice mixture all over the chicken.

5 Grill the chicken for 2 to 3 minutes per side, or until the chicken is cooked through. Transfer the chicken to a cutting board and let rest for about 5 minutes before cutting into thick strips.

6 Serve the fajitas "family style": place the grilled chicken and sautéed pepper mixture on a large serving platter, alongside the warmed tortillas and sliced avocado.

NOTE:

My favorite way to warm tortillas is by wrapping them in aluminum foil and placing them in a 350°F oven for 10 to 15 minutes.

MARYLAND BAY SEASONED CRAB CAKES

When it comes to crab cakes, impressing my Delaware-native dad isn't easy. Having grown up near the Chesapeake Bay, he's particular about his crab cakes. And these have earned his seal of approval! A hallmark of a great crab cake is the minimal use of bread crumbs, just enough to hold its shape, and an abundance of sweet, succulent lump crabmeat. You can't go wrong with iconic Old Bay Seasoning, a beloved seasoning that combines celery salt, paprika, and a mysterious blend of secret spices. Pair these crab cakes with home-made Tartar Sauce (page 46) and a squeeze of fresh lemon for an authentic taste of the Chesapeake Bay.

SERVES 4

PREP TIME: **10 minutes**
COOKING TIME: **12 minutes**
TOTAL TIME: **about 22 minutes, plus chilling time**

¼ cup **Classic Mayonnaise (page 42) or store-bought**
2 tablespoons **unsalted butter, melted**
2 teaspoons **fresh lemon juice**
1 teaspoon **Old Bay Seasoning**
¼ teaspoon **kosher salt**
¼ teaspoon **ground black pepper**
1 **large egg**
1 pound **fresh lump crabmeat**
½ cup **panko bread crumbs**
2 teaspoons **finely chopped fresh parsley**
¼ cup **avocado or sunflower oil**

1 In a large mixing bowl, whisk together the mayonnaise, butter, lemon juice, Old Bay, salt, pepper, and egg. Add the crabmeat, panko, and parsley and gently stir together to combine. Cover tightly with plastic wrap and refrigerator for at least an hour or up to 24 hours.

2 Adjust the oven rack to the middle position and preheat to 350°F. Line a rimmed baking sheet with parchment paper and set aside.

3 Shape the crab mixture into 8 crab cakes (⅓ to ½ cup each) and place on the rimmed baking sheet.

4 Add the oil to a cast-iron pan or nonstick skillet over medium-high heat until hot. Carefully place the crab cakes in two batches in the pan and sear until golden brown on both sides, about 3 minutes per side. Serve immediately.

ADOBO SEASONED CHICKEN WINGS

Who can resist a platter of crispy chicken wings on game night? These aren't your typical buffalo wings; they're an oven-baked version that offers a craveable flavor punch without the hassle of deep frying. The magic lies in the adobo seasoning, a dry rub that showcases pungent garlic and onion, earthy cumin, aromatic oregano, and the brightness of turmeric. These wings are an undeniable hit in my household, drawing everyone to the dinner table—especially my kids!

SERVES 4

PREP TIME: **10 minutes**
COOKING TIME: **40 minutes**
TOTAL TIME: **about 50 minutes**

FOR THE ADOBO SEASONING
(MAKES ABOUT ⅓ CUP)
2 tablespoons granulated garlic
1 tablespoon onion powder
1 tablespoon kosher salt
2 teaspoons dried oregano
1 teaspoon ground cumin
½ teaspoon ground turmeric
½ teaspoon ground black pepper

FOR THE CHICKEN WINGS
3 pounds chicken wings, cut into drumettes and flats
2 tablespoons avocado or sunflower oil
¼ cup adobo seasoning

1 To make the adobo seasoning: Whisk together all the ingredients in a mixing bowl and store in an airtight container until ready to use.

2 To prepare the chicken wings: Adjust an oven rack to the upper middle position and preheat to 425°F. Place a wire rack inside a parchment- or aluminum foil–lined rimmed baking sheet.

3 Thoroughly pat dry the chicken wings with paper towels. Place in a large mixing bowl with the oil and adobo seasoning; toss well to coat. Place the chicken wings on the prepared baking rack, leaving a bit of space between each wing.

4 Bake the wings for 20 minutes. Then flip them over with tongs and bake for another 15 minutes. Flip them back over again and bake them for a final 15 minutes, or until golden brown and crisp. Serve immediately.

CURRIED CHICKEN MEATBALLS
with Spiced Mango Glaze

Who says family dishes can't be vibrant and bold? These meatballs, a unanimous favorite in my household, seamlessly weave the aromatic flavors of curry powder and garam masala into their perfectly moist texture. Fresh cilantro is sprinkled into the mix, complementing the rich spices and adding a burst of freshness to the dish. The meatballs are brushed with a sweet mango glaze that's subtly spiced with a hint of garam masala and a touch of turmeric, and then baked until perfectly golden brown. Enjoy these on their own, or wrap them up in a warm piece of naan slathered with Cucumber Raita (page 52).

SERVES 4

PREP TIME: **15 minutes**
COOKING TIME: **45 minutes**
TOTAL TIME: **about 55 minutes**

FOR THE SPICED MANGO GLAZE
2 cups frozen mango
½ cup granulated sugar
¼ cup water
3 tablespoons fresh lemon juice
½ teaspoon garam masala
¼ teaspoon ground turmeric
¼ teaspoon kosher salt

FOR THE MEATBALLS
2 tablespoons avocado or sunflower oil
½ yellow onion, finely diced
2 garlic cloves, minced or grated
1 pound ground chicken
½ cup panko bread crumbs
¼ cup mango glaze
1 large egg, beaten
2 teaspoons chopped fresh cilantro
1 teaspoon mild curry powder
1 teaspoon kosher salt
½ teaspoon garam masala
½ teaspoon ground black pepper

1. To make the spiced mango glaze: Add all the ingredients to a saucepan over medium-high heat and bring to a boil. Reduce to a simmer and let cook for about 20 minutes, stirring often, until the mixture thickens. Use an immersion blender or high-speed blender to blend until smooth, and allow to cool. This glaze will last for up to a week stored in an airtight container or jar in the refrigerator.

2. To prepare the meatballs: Adjust an oven rack to the middle position and preheat the oven to 375°F. Line a rimmed baking sheet with parchment paper.

3. Add the oil to a saucepan over medium heat. Add the onions and cook for 3 to 4 minutes, until translucent. Add the garlic and cook for another 30 seconds. Remove from the heat and set aside to cool.

4. In a large mixing bowl, combine the remaining ingredients and the cooled onion mixture until well incorporated. Wet your hands and shape the mixture into 16 meatballs, about 2 tablespoons each, and place on the prepared baking sheet.

5. Brush the top of each meatball with the mango glaze and bake for 20 to 25 minutes, or until golden brown on top and the center reaches an internal temperature of 160°F. Serve while warm with a bit of extra mango glaze on the side for dipping.

SOUTHWEST BEEF & ROASTED VEGETABLE CASSEROLE

The defining characteristic of Southwestern cuisine is undoubtedly the presence of chilies, especially green hatch chilies, also known as New Mexican chilies. This recipe seamlessly incorporates these chilies into a boldly spiced beef mixture that features smoky notes of chili powder, earthy cumin, and sweet undertones of paprika. The zesty mixture pairs perfectly with the natural sweetness of the roasted butternut squash and sweet bell pepper. A generous layer of melted mozzarella and spicy pepper jack cheese provides a stretchy, gooey finish. Simply scoop a serving into a bowl for a comforting, complete meal.

SERVES 4

PREP TIME: **10 minutes**
COOKING TIME: **50 minutes**
TOTAL TIME: **about 60 minutes**

FOR THE SPICE BLEND
2 tablespoons chili powder
1 tablespoon ground cumin
1 tablespoon sweet paprika
1 tablespoon granulated garlic
2 teaspoons kosher salt
1 teaspoon ground coriander
1 teaspoon dried oregano
½ teaspoon ground black pepper
¼ teaspoon cayenne pepper

FOR THE CASSEROLE
1 pound butternut squash, peeled, seeded, and diced
1 large red bell pepper, seeded and diced
4 tablespoons avocado or sunflower oil
½ medium yellow onion
2 garlic cloves, minced
1 pound ground beef
2 Roma tomatoes, diced
One 4-ounce can diced green chilies
2 cups stemmed and chopped curly kale
Kosher salt, as needed
1 cup shredded low-moisture mozzarella cheese
1 cup shredded pepper jack cheese

1   To make the spice blend: Whisk together all the ingredients in a mixing bowl. Store in an airtight container until ready to use.

2   To prepare the casserole: Adjust the oven rack to the middle position and heat to 400°F. Line a rimmed baking sheet with parchment paper.

3   Add the butternut squash and the bell pepper to the prepared baking sheet and drizzle with 2 tablespoons of the oil and 1 tablespoon of the spice blend, tossing well to coat. Arrange in a single layer and roast in the oven for about 25 minutes, or until the butternut squash is tender and lightly browned. (Leave the oven on to bake the casserole.)

4   While the vegetables are roasting, heat the remaining 2 tablespoons of oil in a sauté pan over medium-high heat. Add the onions and cook for about 3 minutes or until tender and translucent. Add the garlic and cook for another 30 seconds or so. Add the ground beef to the onion mixture and cook until the beef is no longer pink and browned all the way through, about 5 minutes. Drain the beef if excess grease has accumulated in the pan. Add 2 tablespoons of the spice blend, the diced tomatoes, diced green chilies, and kale. Stir to combine and cook for another 5 minutes, or until the kale is wilted. Taste the mixture for seasoning, adding more salt if needed.

5   Transfer the meat mixture to an 8-by-8-inch baking dish and top with the roasted vegetables. Sprinkle the shredded mozzarella and pepper jack cheeses over the top.

6   Bake in the oven for 20 to 25 minutes, or until the cheese is melted on top. Serve immediately.

CHAPTER 9

SOMETHING
SWEET

Desserts, just like savory dishes, offer an opportunity to explore new flavor profiles and push the boundaries of creativity. They are not solely meant to satisfy a sweet tooth but can also encompass a wide range of taste sensations, including salty, sour, bitter, and umami flavors. The recipes in this chapter incorporate ingredients that go beyond sweetness, such as white miso and citrus zest, to add depth and complexity to the desserts.

A delightful spice blend can transform a simple cake into a flavor-packed delight, and the process of browning butter can introduce an irresistible nuttiness and an extra layer of indulgence to various sweet treats. While desserts can be as simple as farm-fresh strawberries with a dollop of homemade whipped cream, the goal of the recipes in this chapter is to elevate these familiar desserts by exploring a variety of flavors and techniques. This collection of recipes caters to various skill levels. Approachable options for novice bakers include Butterscotch Banana Bread Cookies (page 194) and Vovó's Blueberry Cake (page 199), and more advanced bakers can seek a greater challenge with recipes like Winter Pavlova with Mixed Citrus Curd (page 206).

My Portuguese heritage and cherished memories of cooking alongside my vovó as a child inspired many of the recipes here, including Almost-Burnt Caramel Flan (page 204), Cinnamon-Infused Sweet Rice Pudding (page 203), and Fried Malasada with Vanilla Bean Sugar (page 210). With their rich use of eggs, particularly egg yolks and sugar, Portuguese desserts have earned a reputation for their distinctive sweet, custard-like flavor. In addition to Feast & Fettle favorites such as the Chocolate-Covered Brown Butter Crispy Rice Treats (page 200) and Miso White Chocolate Chip Cookies (page 196), you'll discover other recipes that embrace the leveled-up flavor themes of this cookbook, such as the Matcha Basque-Style Cheesecake with Strawberry Compote (page 214).

BUTTERSCOTCH BANANA BREAD COOKIES

When I find myself craving the comforting flavors of banana bread but only have a single brown banana on hand (you need at least three for a full loaf), I turn to these soft and chewy banana bread cookies. This recipe offers a delicious twist on the classic recipe, and bakes in a fraction of the time. The use of brown butter elevates the flavor profile, infusing the dough with a luscious nuttiness. The combination of mashed ripe banana and dark brown sugar provides just the right amount of sweetness while ensuring a tender and moist crumb. And the inclusion of butterscotch chips introduces a delightful caramel undertone to each bite.

MAKES 9 LARGE COOKIES

PREP TIME: **10 minutes**
COOKING TIME: **20 minutes**
TOTAL TIME: **about 1 hour, includes dough chilling time**

FOR THE BROWN BUTTER
½ cup (115 g) unsalted butter, sliced

FOR THE COOKIES
1½ cups (190 g) all-purpose flour
½ teaspoon baking soda
1 teaspoon ground cinnamon
½ teaspoon (2 g) kosher salt
⅓ cup (100 g) mashed ripe banana
¾ cup (146 g) dark or light brown sugar, packed
1 egg yolk
1 teaspoon vanilla extract
¾ cup (120 g) butterscotch chips

1 Make the brown butter: In a stainless steel saucepan or skillet over medium heat, melt the butter until it starts to foam, stirring constantly with a wooden spoon or rubber spatula during the process.

2 After a few minutes the butter will foam, then turn a light golden brown and start to smell intensely nutty. Once the milk solids have turned medium brown, immediately remove the pan from the heat and pour into a heatproof bowl to stop the cooking process. From start to finish this process should take 7 to 8 minutes. Set aside to cool slightly.

3 Make the cookies: In a small mixing bowl, whisk together the flour, baking soda, cinnamon, and salt. Set aside.

4 In a large mixing bowl, whisk together the banana, melted brown butter, dark brown sugar, egg yolk, and vanilla. Then add the dry ingredients and stir until just combined and no streaks of flour remain. Fold in the butterscotch chips until incorporated.

5 Cover the cookie dough tightly and place in the refrigerator for at least 30 minutes or up to 24 hours, which allows the dough to chill and prevents the cookies from spreading too much when baked. During the chilling process, set baking racks in the top third and bottom third of the oven, preheat to 350°F, and line 2 rimmed baking sheets with parchment paper.

6 Using a large cookie scoop or measuring spoon, scoop about 3 tablespoons of cookie dough per cookie and place on the baking sheets, making sure to leave space between each cookie. I like to bake 6 large cookie dough balls on one baking sheet and the remaining 3 on the other.

7 Bake the cookies for 11 to 13 minutes, or until the edges are set but the middle is still soft, rotating the pans halfway though baking. Allow the cookies to cool on the baking sheet for about 10 minutes before transferring them to a wire rack to cool completely. These cookies will keep for about a week stored in an airtight container at room temperature.

NOTES:

- ⅓ cup mashed ripe banana is equal to one small ripe banana.
- You can substitute melted butter for the brown butter in this recipe, but the flavor will be slightly different, as the brown butter adds a delicious nuttiness to the cookies.
- Feel free to substitute chocolate chips for the butterscotch chips.

MISO WHITE CHOCOLATE CHIP COOKIES

During the early years of Feast & Fettle, I developed this irresistible twist on a classic chocolate chip cookie recipe that has since become a beloved favorite. Inspired by my appreciation for the combination of flaky sea salt and chocolate chip cookies, this recipe takes a unique approach: It incorporates white miso into the cookie dough to impart a savory saltiness. The result is a perfect harmony between the sweet, buttery flavor of white chocolate and the subtle umami notes of the white miso. The combination of melted butter and chilling the dough yields cookies with perfectly golden-brown edges and an irresistible soft and chewy texture.

MAKES 14 LARGE COOKIES

PREP TIME: **10 minutes**
COOKING TIME: **25 minutes**
TOTAL TIME: **about 1 hour 5 minutes**, includes dough chilling time

2 cups (260 g) all-purpose flour
1 teaspoon baking powder
1 teaspoon baking soda
½ teaspoon (2 g) kosher salt
¾ cup (170 g) unsalted butter, cubed
¾ cup (160 g) light brown sugar
¼ cup (50 g) granulated sugar
2 tablespoons (36 g) white miso
1 large egg, room temperature
1 egg yolk
1 teaspoon vanilla extract
1½ cups (275 g) white chocolate chips

NOTE:

- To bring eggs to room temperature quickly, place whole eggs in a glass of warm water for about 5 minutes.

1 In a medium mixing bowl, whisk together the flour, baking powder, baking soda, and salt. Set aside.

2 Melt the butter in a small saucepan over medium-low heat until just melted. Set aside to cool for about 5 minutes.

3 Add the melted butter, brown sugar, granulated sugar, and miso to the bowl of a stand mixer fitted with the paddle attachment. Beat together on medium-low speed for about 2 minutes. Meanwhile, add the egg, egg yolk, and vanilla to a small bowl and beat with a fork until combined.

4 Add the egg mixture to the wet mixture and beat on slow speed until combined, about 30 seconds.

5 Add the flour mixture to the wet mixture and slowly beat until just combined. Add the white chocolate chips and beat for another 30 seconds until incorporated. Cover the cookie dough with plastic wrap and refrigerate for at least 1 hour and up to 24 hours.

6 Set baking racks in the top third and bottom third of the oven and preheat to 350°F. Line two rimmed sheet pans with parchment paper and set aside.

7 Using a large cookie scoop, about 3 tablespoons, scoop out dough onto the prepared sheet pans, making sure to leave space between each cookie—I can typically fit 8 cookies on a sheet pan.

8 Bake the cookies for 12 to 14 minutes, or until golden brown at the edge and still soft in the center, rotating the pans halfway through baking. These will keep for about a week at room temperature when stored in an airtight container.

VOVÓ'S BLUEBERRY CAKE

I cherish vivid memories from my childhood, summers spent with my cousins darting beneath the nets of my grandparents' eight bountiful blueberry bushes to gather handfuls of fruit. Each season, my vovó would transform these freshly picked blueberries into delicious pies and baked goods. This particular cake, however, holds a special place in my heart as it always brings back fond memories of her. While this recipe essentially mirrors a classic blueberry buckle, my vovó put her unique spin on it. The key difference lies in her addition of fresh blueberries to the buttery spiced crumb topping, instead of using the crumb alone. The fresh blueberries add a burst of vibrant flavor, their slight tartness contrasting beautifully with the cake's inherent sweetness.

SERVES 9 TO 12

PREP TIME: **15 minutes**
COOKING TIME: **60 minutes**
TOTAL TIME: **about 1 hour
15 minutes, plus cooling time**

FOR THE TOPPING
½ cup (60 g) all-purpose flour
½ cup (100 g) granulated sugar
½ teaspoon ground cinnamon
⅛ teaspoon ground nutmeg
5 tablespoons (70 g) cold unsalted butter, cubed
2 cups (380 g) blueberries

FOR THE CAKE
2 cups (260 g) all-purpose flour
2 teaspoons baking powder
½ teaspoon (2 g) salt
½ cup (113 g) unsalted butter, softened
¾ cup (150 g) granulated sugar
2 large eggs, beaten
1 teaspoon vanilla extract
½ cup (120 ml) whole milk
1 cup (190 g) blueberries

1 First, make the topping: In a small mixing bowl, combine the flour, sugar, cinnamon, and nutmeg. Cut or rub in the butter with your fingers or a pastry cutter until it reaches a crumbly state.

2 Gently stir in the blueberries and set aside.

3 To prepare the cake: Adjust the oven rack to the center position and preheat to 375°F. Grease a 9-by-9-inch baking pan. Line the baking pan with a piece of parchment paper long enough to cover the bottom of the pan with a bit extra hanging over the sides (this will help to easily remove the cake from the pan after baking).

4 In a medium mixing bowl, whisk together the flour, baking powder, and salt. Set aside.

5 Add the softened butter and sugar to the bowl of a stand mixer fitted with the paddle attachment (alternatively using a hand mixer) and beat until pale yellow and creamy, about 2 minutes, scraping down the sides of the bowl as needed. Then add the eggs and vanilla and beat on medium speed for another 30 seconds or until combined.

6 Add half of the flour mixture to the wet ingredients and beat on low speed until just incorporated. Add the milk and the remaining flour and continue to beat on low speed until just combined, about 1 minute. Be careful not to overmix the batter. Gently stir in the blueberries. This batter is very thick.

7 Transfer the batter into the prepared baking pan and top with the blueberry crumb topping. Bake for 55 to 60 minutes, or until a cake tester or toothpick comes out clean.

8 Let the cake cool on a wire rack for 15 to 30 minutes before gently removing from the pan and serving.

CHOCOLATE-COVERED BROWN BUTTER CRISPY RICE TREATS

A version of these crispy rice treats, inspired by Smitten Kitchen's Salted Brown Butter Crispy Treats, holds a special place in my heart, as it was the very first dessert I put on a Feast & Fettle menu. I have fond memories making countless batches of this popular treat in the early years of the company. While crispy rice treats may not typically be associated with fancy desserts, the addition of nutty brown butter, a rich chocolate layer, and a sprinkle of flaky sea salt brings a touch of sophistication to this beloved classic.

MAKES 9 LARGE SQUARES

PREP TIME: **5 minutes**
COOKING TIME: **15 minutes**
TOTAL TIME: about **20 minutes**, plus cooling time

FOR THE TREATS
½ cup (113 g) unsalted butter
One 10-ounce (283 g) bag mini marshmallows, reserve ½ cup
6 cups (170 g) Rice Krispies cereal
½ teaspoon (2 g) kosher salt

FOR THE CHOCOLATE TOPPING
8 ounces (228 g) semi-sweet chocolate bar, roughly chopped
1 to 2 teaspoons (4 to 8 g) Maldon Sea Salt Flakes

NOTES:

- You can substitute melted butter for the brown butter, but the flavor will be slightly different, as the brown butter adds a delicious nuttiness.

- You can substitute regular-sized marshmallows for the mini marshmallows, but increase the amount to 12 ounces.

1. To make the treats: Grease an 8-by-8-inch square baking pan and set aside.

2. In a large pot over medium heat, melt the butter until it starts to foam, stirring constantly with a wooden spoon or rubber spatula.

3. After a few minutes the butter will turn a light golden brown and start to smell intensely nutty. Once the milk solids have turned medium brown, immediately lower the heat and stir in the marshmallows until completely smooth, then turn off the heat.

4. Add the rice cereal, salt, and the reserved ½ cup of marshmallows to the pot and stir until combined.

5. While still warm, transfer the mixture to the prepared baking pan. Lightly and evenly press into the pan. Set aside to cool.

6. To make the chocolate topping: Place the chocolate in a microwave-safe bowl and heat for 1 minute on high. Stir and then microwave in 20-second intervals until completely smooth.

7. Pour the melted chocolate over the top of the crispy rice treats and evenly spread out with a small offset spatula or spoon. Sprinkle the Maldon sea salt over the top of the chocolate and let sit until the chocolate has hardened.

8. Remove from the pan and transfer to a cutting board. Cut into a 3-by-3-inch grid to get 9 large squares. These treats will keep for about a week stored in an airtight container at room temperature.

CINNAMON-INFUSED SWEET RICE PUDDING

Crafted from humble ingredients, this sweet and creamy dessert, also known as arroz doce, captures the essence of traditional Portuguese sweets. Fragrant cinnamon sticks and lemon peel infuse the milk, imparting a hint of warm spice and bright citrus notes that beautifully complement the creamy rice base. The addition of velvety egg yolks at the end gives the pudding a luscious custard-like texture and further enhances its rich flavor. Each spoonful of this nostalgic dish, often served at Portuguese family gatherings, evokes fond childhood memories. The versatility of rice pudding shines, as it can be enjoyed warm or chilled, making it the perfect indulgence year-round.

SERVES 6

PREP TIME: **10 minutes**
COOKING TIME: **40 minutes**
TOTAL TIME: **about 50 minutes, plus chilling time**

- **2 cups (474 ml) water**
- **½ teaspoon (2 g) kosher salt**
- **1 cup (190 g) white rice, medium grain such as River Rice**
- **3 cups (720 ml) whole milk, plus more if needed**
- **¾ cup (150 g) granulated sugar**
- **2 cinnamon sticks**
- **½ teaspoon vanilla extract**
- **2 large lemon or orange rind strips**
- **2 egg yolks, beaten**
- **1 to 2 teaspoons ground cinnamon**

1. In a medium saucepan, bring the water and salt to a boil. Add the rice, cover, and reduce the heat to low. Cook for 15 minutes.

2. Add the milk, sugar, cinnamon sticks, vanilla, and lemon rind to the rice. Increase the heat to medium and bring to a boil. Then reduce the heat to low and simmer for about 25 minutes, stirring frequently, until the mixture has thickened.

3. Turn off the heat and vigorously stir in the beaten egg yolks. Remove the cinnamon stick and lemon rind from the rice mixture before transferring to a casserole or serving dish and sprinkling the cinnamon over the top.

4. Serve warm or refrigerate for at least an hour to serve chilled. This dish will keep for up to 5 days in an airtight container in the refrigerator.

NOTES:

- If the rice mixture becomes too thick while simmering, add another 2 to 4 tablespoons of milk.
- The heat from the rice mixture will cook the raw egg yolks.

ALMOST-BURNT CARAMEL FLAN

Essentially just eggs, milk, and sugar, flan exemplifies the marriage of simplicity and technique. The art of creating the perfect flan lies in the meticulous execution of each step, ensuring the perfect balance of flavors and the desired velvety texture. In this version, I take the caramelization process well beyond the golden stage until a deep amber hue is achieved. This technique captures the essence of almost-burnt sugar and infuses the entire custard with an irresistible, complex caramel flavor.

SERVES 6 TO 8

PREP TIME: **10 minutes**
COOKING TIME: **1 hour 25 minutes**
TOTAL TIME: **about 1 hour 35 minutes, plus chilling time**

FOR THE CARAMEL
¾ cup (150 g) sugar
¼ cup (60 g) water

FOR THE CUSTARD
3 large eggs
3 egg yolks
One 14-ounce (396 g) can sweetened condensed milk
One 12-ounce (354 ml) can evaporated milk
¼ cup (60 ml) half-and-half or whole milk
1 tablespoon vanilla extract
½ teaspoon (2 g) kosher salt

1   To make the caramel: Combine the sugar and water in a saucepan over medium-high heat. Swirl the pan a bit to incorporate and dissolve the sugar. Bring the mixture to a boil. Lower the heat to medium-low and continue to cook. Gently swirl the pan and brush the sides with water as needed until the caramel is fragrant and reaches a deep amber color, then immediately turn off the heat (see Note). This process should take 7 to 8 minutes.

2   Pour the caramel syrup into the bottom of an 8½-by-5-inch glass loaf pan and set aside.

3   To make the custard: Preheat the oven to 325°F and set the oven rack to the middle position.

4   Whisk the eggs and yolks together in a large mixing bowl. Then add the sweetened condensed milk, evaporated milk, half-and-half, vanilla, and salt and whisk until fully incorporated.

5   Strain the mixture through a fine-mesh strainer into another large bowl, ensuring a smooth custard by removing any bits of egg that didn't fully incorporate. Pour the strained custard into the loaf pan over the top of the caramel. Cover tightly with aluminum foil.

6   Place the loaf pan in the center of a large 9-by-13-inch baking pan and place in the oven. Pour boiling hot water into the large baking dish, surrounding the loaf pan until it reaches about halfway up the loaf pan. Bake for 70 to 80 minutes. The custard should be fully set around the edges and the center should be slightly jiggly.

7   Remove the loaf pan from the water bath and wipe dry. Allow the flan to cool for about 1 hour at room temperature before covering it or wrapping it in plastic wrap and refrigerating for at least 4 hours but preferably overnight.

8   When ready to serve, carefully slide a thin sharp knife or offset spatula around the edge of the loaf pan. Carefully invert the flan onto a rimmed serving platter. Slice the flan into individual portions and spoon extra caramel sauce over the top. This dish will last for up to 4 days stored in an airtight container in the refrigerator.

NOTE:

It's important not to stir the caramel with a whisk or spoon during the caramelization process; gently swirling the pan is sufficient.

WINTER PAVLOVA
with Mixed Citrus Curd

This delightfully crisp but ever-so-slightly chewy dessert is the perfect complement to a heavy winter meal. It is composed of a meringue that has a crunchy outer shell and a soft marshmallow-like texture on the inside. The pavlova (meringue), which can be made ahead of time, is then smothered with fresh whipped cream and a tangy, thick citrus curd, and then piled high with juicy blackberries and sweet mandarins. This dessert is the ultimate showstopper with its billowy cloud-like base and colorful fresh fruit toppings.

SERVES 8

PREP TIME: **30 minutes**
COOKING TIME: **1 hour 30 minutes**
TOTAL TIME: **about 4 hours,**
including cooling time

FOR THE PAVLOVA
4 large egg whites, room temperature
⅛ teaspoon kosher salt
½ teaspoon cream of tartar
1 cup (225 g) superfine or quick-dissolve sugar
1 teaspoon cornstarch
½ teaspoon vanilla extract

FOR THE CURD
1 cup (200 g) granulated sugar
1 tablespoon (6 g) orange zest
1 tablespoon (6 g) lemon zest
4 large egg yolks
1 large egg
¼ cup (60 ml) fresh orange juice
¼ cup (60 ml) fresh lemon juice
½ cup (113 g) unsalted butter, cold, cubed

FOR THE WHIPPED CREAM
1 cup (240 g) heavy whipping cream
¼ cup (25 g) confectioners' sugar
½ teaspoon vanilla extract

FOR THE TOPPING
½ cup (70 g) blackberries
1 mandarin or clementine, peeled and sliced into wheels

1   To make the pavlova: Heat the oven to 350°F. Line a large baking sheet with parchment paper and set aside.

2   In the bowl of an electric mixer fitted with the whisk attachment, begin to beat the egg whites and salt at a low speed, gradually increasing the speed to medium-high, beating until soft peaks are achieved. Add the cream of tartar and beat for 30 seconds before adding the superfine sugar in a slow, steady stream. Turn the mixture up to high and continue beating until the meringue is very stiff and shiny. The peaks should be stiff enough to hold the whisk attachment upright without the peaks moving. Sprinkle the cornstarch and vanilla over the meringue and gently fold with a rubber spatula.

3   Mound the meringue onto the parchment paper and spread into an 8- or 9-inch circle, making decorative peaks around the edges and sides as you smooth down the top.

4   Place the pavlova in the oven, drop the oven temperature to 250°F, and continue baking for about 70 minutes. Turn off the heat and let the meringue cool completely in the oven. Once cool, the pavlova can be wrapped and stored at room temperature for up to 2 days.

5   To make the curd: Add the sugar, orange zest, lemon zest, egg yolks, whole egg, and citrus juices to a medium stainless steel saucepan and whisk to combine. Over medium-low heat, continue whisking the curd, cooking it until it becomes thick and able to coat the back of a wooden spoon, 8 to 10 minutes.

6   Remove from the heat and slowly whisk in the butter until melted and fully incorporated.

7   Using a rubber spatula, push the curd mixture through a fine mesh strainer and into a small mixing bowl to remove any egg bits or larger pieces of citrus zest, ensuring the curd is silky smooth.

8   Let the curd cool slightly, then transfer into an airtight container and refrigerate; it will continue to thicken as it cools. The curd will last for up to 2 weeks stored in an airtight container in the refrigerator.

9   To make the whipped cream: Place the metal bowl of stand mixer in the freezer for 10 to 15 minutes to chill.

10 Add the heavy cream, confectioners' sugar, and vanilla to the cold metal bowl; using the whisk attachment, start whipping the cream until medium-to-stiff peaks form. Use immediately or store in an airtight container in the refrigerator for up to 12 hours.

11 To assemble: Place the pavlova on a serving dish or platter and top with whipped cream, then layer the citrus curd over the top. Decorate with blackberries and sliced mandarins. Slice and serve immediately.

NOTES:

- Cold eggs are easier to separate, but for faster whipping, let the egg whites sit at room temperature for 10 minutes before whipping.

- It is normal for the pavlova to have light cracking once completely cooled.

Winter Pavlova

FRIED MALASADA
with Vanilla Bean Sugar

In 2016, my best friend Nicole Nix made the bold decision to leave her hospitality position and join me in launching Feast & Fettle. Throughout our friendship, we have always shared a deep connection rooted in our Portuguese heritage and love for its rich culinary traditions. One particular treat that holds a special place in our hearts is malasada, or Portuguese fried dough. With just one bite of the fluffy yeasted dough coated in a generous layer of granulated sugar, we are instantly transported back to our cherished childhood memories of Portuguese festivals and family gatherings. Infusing the finishing sugar with fragrant vanilla bean adds just a touch of unexpected sophistication to this timeless recipe.

MAKES 18 TO 20 MALASADA

PREP TIME: **30 minutes**
RISE TIME: **2 hours 30 minutes**
COOKING TIME: **35 minutes**
TOTAL TIME: **3 hours 35 minutes**

FOR THE VANILLA BEAN SUGAR
1 cup (200 g) granulated sugar
1 vanilla bean

FOR THE DOUGH
2¼ teaspoons (1 packet) instant yeast
¼ cup (50 g) plus 1 teaspoon (4 g) granulated sugar
2 tablespoons (30 g) warm water, 110°F
½ cup (120 ml) whole milk
3 tablespoons (43 g) unsalted butter
½ teaspoon (2 g) kosher salt
4 large eggs, room temperature
3½ cups (450 g) all-purpose flour, more if needed
Cooking spray
40 ounces or 5 cups (1.25 L) avocado or sunflower oil

1 To make the vanilla bean sugar: Add the sugar to the bowl of a food processor fitted with the S blade.

2 Cut the vanilla bean in half lengthwise and use the knife to scrape out the seeds from the pod. Add the seeds to the sugar. Pulse until incorporated into the sugar. Pour the flavored sugar into a glass jar with a tight-fitting lid and set aside.

3 Next, make the dough. In a small bowl, dissolve the yeast and 1 teaspoon of the sugar in the warm water. Loosely cover with a clean kitchen towel and set aside for 10 minutes until foamy on top.

4 Heat the milk, butter, and salt in a medium saucepan over medium heat, until the butter melts and small bubbles begin to form. Remove from the heat and let cool until lukewarm.

5 In the bowl of a stand mixer fitted with the paddle attachment, beat the eggs and the ¼ cup sugar on high speed until thick and creamy, 4 to 5 minutes.

6 Switch to the dough hook, add the milk mixture, yeast mixture, and flour and knead on medium-low speed for 5 to 6 minutes, or until a soft dough forms. Add an additional 1 to 2 tablespoons of flour if needed. The dough should be soft and somewhat sticky.

7 Transfer the dough using a dough scraper or rubber spatula to a lightly buttered medium mixing bowl and cover tightly with plastic wrap. Allow the dough to rise in a relatively warm spot for about 2 hours, or until it doubles in size.

8   Spray a rimmed baking sheet with cooking spray. Punch down the dough to release the air, divide into 18 to 20 equal portions, and place on the prepared baking sheet. Lightly spray the top of the dough with cooking spray and loosely cover with plastic wrap. Let the dough rest at room temperature for about 30 minutes.

9   Set up a rimmed baking sheet lined with paper towels and set aside. Pour ½ cup of the vanilla sugar into a large shallow bowl and set aside.

10 Pour the oil into a large, thick-bottomed pot or Dutch oven over medium-high heat. Heat the oil to 350°F. Lightly stretch and flatten the dough into a 4-inch circle before carefully adding to the hot oil 2 or 3 at a time. Fry until just golden brown, about 1 minute per side. Carefully remove with a wire spider strainer or large slotted spoon and place on the paper towel–lined baking sheet to drain. While still warm, toss in the vanilla sugar to coat on all sides. Repeat with the remaining dough, then turn off the heat. Serve immediately or store in an airtight container for up to 2 days.

NOTES:

- Substitute 2 to 3 tablespoons of lemon zest for the vanilla bean to make a lemon-flavored sugar.

- Lightly rubbing your hands in oil will help when handling the dough.

- Use a deep-fry thermometer, candy thermometer, or instant-read thermometer to monitor the oil temperature during the frying process.

- To make overnight: Prepare the dough but instead of letting it rise in a warm environment, place it in the refrigerator overnight for 8 to 12 hours. In the morning, remove the dough from the refrigerator and let it rise in a warm environment until it doubles in size and then continue with the recipe as provided here.

CHOCOLATE TRES LECHES CAKE

Tres leches cake, literally translated as "three milks cake," is one of my all-time favorites to bake for special occasions and gatherings. Traditionally the recipe boasts a perfectly moist sponge cake that's infused with a luscious syrup of three milks, vanilla, and cinnamon. With this recipe I wanted to take it a step further and create an even more indulgent treat by incorporating the rich flavor of chocolate. The light chocolate sponge cake, created by folding whipped egg whites into the batter and infusing chocolate in the three-milks syrup, combine to enhance the overall decadent nature of this cake.

SERVES 12

PREP TIME: **25 minutes**
COOKING TIME: **30 minutes**
TOTAL TIME: **55 minutes**

FOR THE CAKE
1 cup (125 g) all-purpose flour
¼ cup (50 g) cocoa powder
1½ teaspoons baking powder
¼ teaspoon kosher salt
5 large eggs, separated
1 cup (200 g) sugar
½ cup (125 g) chocolate milk
1 teaspoon vanilla extract

FOR THE SYRUP
**One 12-ounce (354 ml) can
  evaporated milk**
**One 14-ounce (396 g) can sweetened
  condensed milk**
¼ cup (60 ml) chocolate milk

FOR THE TOPPING
**2 cups (480 ml) heavy whipping
  cream**
½ cup (50 g) confectioners' sugar
One 3-ounce (85 g) chocolate bar

1 To make the cake: Adjust the oven rack to the middle position and preheat to 350°F. Grease a 9-by-13-inch glass baking dish or casserole pan.

2 In a large bowl, whisk together the flour, cocoa powder, baking powder, and salt. Set aside.

3 Add the egg yolks and ¾ cup of the sugar to the bowl of a stand mixer fitted with the paddle attachment (alternatively using a hand mixer) and beat on high speed until the yolks turn a pale yellow color, about 2 minutes. Add the chocolate milk and vanilla and beat for another 30 seconds. Pour the egg mixture over the top of the flour mixture and gently stir to combine.

4 Add the egg whites to the bowl of a stand mixer fitted with the whisk attachment (alternatively using a hand mixer) and whip on medium-high speed until soft peaks form. Slowly add the remaining ¼ cup sugar, continuing to beat on high until stiff peaks form, which should take 4 to 5 minutes.

5 Add the stiff egg whites to the batter and gently fold with a rubber spatula until just combined. Try to not overmix.

6 Pour the batter into the prepared baking dish and smooth out the top. Bake for 30 minutes, or until a toothpick or cake tester comes out clean. Set aside to cool.

7 To make the syrup: Combine the evaporated milk, condensed milk, and chocolate milk in a small mixing bowl.

8 Once the cake has cooled, use a fork or chopstick to poke holes all over the top. Slowly pour 3 cups of the milk syrup mixture over the

top of the cake, allowing it to soak in for at least 15 minutes or up to overnight before topping with whipped cream.

9 For the topping, add the heavy whipping cream and confectioners' sugar to the bowl of a stand mixer fitted with the whisk attachment (alternatively using a hand mixer) and whip on medium-high speed until stiff peaks form, which should take 3 to 4 minutes.

10 Using an offset spatula or large spoon, spread the whipped cream topping all over the top of the cake. Shave the edge of the chocolate bar with a vegetable peeler into a small bowl and sprinkle the chocolate shavings all over the top of the cake. This cake will last for up to 3 days stored in an airtight container in the refrigerator.

NOTE:

Cold eggs are easier to separate, but for faster whipping, let the egg whites sit at room temperature for 10 minutes before whipping.

MATCHA BASQUE-STYLE CHEESECAKE
with Strawberry Compote

Basque cheesecake, renowned for its deeply browned top and tantalizing creamy center, is achieved by baking at an exceptionally high temperature—a method much simpler than its American counterpart, as it bypasses the need for a water bath and cuts down on the baking time. My rendition of this classic incorporates matcha, which infuses the cheesecake with a vibrant green hue. The earthy flavors of matcha meld beautifully with the rich, creamy sweetness of the cheesecake, creating a flavor profile that's both complex and delightfully unexpected. A sweet, tangy strawberry compote finishes off the dish, adding a brilliant red pop of color and a lively counterpoint to the cheesecake's luscious creaminess.

SERVES 8 TO 10

PREP TIME: **25 minutes**
COOKING TIME: **50 minutes**
TOTAL TIME: **1 hour 15 minutes, plus cooling time**

FOR THE CHEESECAKE
2 pounds (908 g) full-fat cream cheese, room temperature

1½ cups (300 g) granulated sugar

¼ cup (19 g) matcha powder

½ teaspoon (2 g) kosher salt

6 large eggs, room temperature

1 cup (240 ml) heavy cream

1 teaspoon vanilla extract

2 tablespoons (15 g) all-purpose flour

FOR THE COMPOTE
1 pound (450 g) fresh strawberries, hulled and halved

¼ cup (50 g) granulated sugar

1 tablespoon (15 g) fresh lemon juice

1   To make the cheesecake: Set the baking rack in the center of the oven and preheat the oven to 425°F. Take two sheets of parchment paper, about 13 by 15 inches each, crossing one over the top of the other and press them into the bottom of a lightly greased 9-inch springform pan, making sure to completely cover the bottom and sides of the pan. Fold the excess parchment over the sides of the pan.

2   Add the cream cheese to the bowl of a stand mixer fitted with the paddle attachment (alternatively using a hand mixer) and beat on high speed for 1 minute until completely smooth.

3   Add the sugar, matcha powder, and salt and beat on medium speed for another minute or so, making sure to scrape down the sides as needed. Add the eggs one at a time, on medium speed until incorporated. Carefully add the heavy cream and vanilla, beating on medium-low speed until smooth, about 30 seconds, again scraping down the sides as needed.

4   Sift the flour over the cream cheese mixture and beat on medium-low speed until incorporated and smooth, about 30 seconds.

5   Pour the mixture into the prepared springform pan and bake for 40 minutes. Then turn up the heat to 500°F and bake for another 5 to 7 minutes, until the top is deeply browned and the center is still quite jiggly. Let cool on the counter for about an hour before transferring to the refrigerator to cool completely.

6   To make the compote: While the cheesecake is baking, combine the strawberries, sugar, and lemon juice in a small saucepan. Bring to a simmer over medium heat and let cook for about 20 minutes, stirring frequently and mashing up the strawberries as they cook. Let cool and set aside. This compote will keep for up a week stored in an airtight container.

7   Release the cheesecake from the springform pan and peel the parchment away from the sides. Then slice into wedges and serve with the strawberry compote. This cheesecake will last for up to 5 days tightly wrapped or stored in an airtight container in the refrigerator.

NOTES:

- You can substitute frozen strawberries for fresh strawberries; don't thaw.
- You can omit the matcha powder for a traditional Basque cheesecake.
- This recipe easily can be made gluten-free by substituting a gluten-free flour blend for the all-purpose flour.

ACKNOWLEDGMENTS

Writing a cookbook has always been a dream of mine, although I never actually thought I could do it. When I transitioned from my operational role at Feast & Fettle, the opportunity to fulfill this aspiration became possible—it was a now-or-never moment for me. Writing this cookbook has been the undertaking of a lifetime, and the contents of these pages wouldn't have come to life without the unwavering support of many. They are:

JAMES JAYO, ISABEL McCARTHY, ALLISON CHI, AND THE ENTIRE TEAM AT COUNTRYMAN PRESS, your belief in me and this book means the world. Your unwavering support and guidance throughout this entire process have been truly appreciated. Thank you for taking a chance on this project and making it come to life.

KIM LINDMAN, your encouragement and expert guidance as a first-time author have been invaluable to me throughout this process. Thank you for believing in this project from the very beginning.

KRISTEN TEIG, CATRINE KELTY, AND ERIN McGINN, my dream team for the cookbook photoshoot, I couldn't be happier with the photos in this book. It was an honor to have worked with you all on this project.

CHRISTINE CHITNIS, thank you for being my guiding light and friend throughout this book-writing journey. Your guidance and encouragement pushed my writing to be the best it could be, and I couldn't have completed this book without you.

NICOLE (NIKKI) NIX, my bonus sister, you have supported me in more ways than I can thank you for. From the moment I shared my plan for Feast & Fettle you have been with me every step of the way, and I wouldn't have come this far without you.

CARLOS VENTURA, at a pivotal moment, you took a chance on both me and Feast & Fettle. Had you not, this book would have never been written. Thank you for recognizing my strengths and encouraging me to delve into them. LFG.

KYLA HANAWAY-QUINLAN, I am forever grateful for your support, dedication, and willingness to take the lead on collaborating on this project with me.

THE FEAST & FETTLE TEAM, your unwavering support and encouragement throughout the process of writing this book have meant the world to me. This book wouldn't have been possible without each and every one of you, and I'm deeply grateful for the passion you bring to this company every day.

ALLYSON RAMOS AND HELEN LISTER, your invaluable support and assistance during the cookbook photoshoot made all the difference. Allyson, your dedication to testing every recipe and providing detailed feedback was truly appreciated.

ANNA KENDRICK AND SHEILA BUCKLEY, thank you for enthusiastically testing many of the recipes in this book; your detailed feedback was incredibly valuable.

PETER KING, thank you for allowing us to shoot some of the photos for this book at Chase Cove Cottage. I truly appreciate it.

AUNT MARTHA AND AUNT MARIA, thank you for sharing Vovó's handwritten recipes with me, and for your encouragement and support during the entire process of writing this book.

AMY AND JON, your unwavering support and enthusiasm for this project are deeply appreciated. Thank you for being there every step of the way.

MOM, your support throughout this journey has been invaluable. From providing me a cozy retreat to write to assisting with the boys to graciously allowing me to take over your house for my photoshoot, you've been there for it all. Love you! Thanks!

DAD, thank you for the constant advice, encouragement, and belief in what I can achieve. Love you!

QUINTIN AND DESMOND, you are my everything. I've worked tirelessly, driven by my desire to make you proud. I hope we will cook out of this book together, creating countless memories in the kitchen. Many recipes in these pages were inspired by you, and you both continue to inspire me every single day. I love you so much!

KYLE, how can words adequately thank someone who has held my hand the entire way? You've been my pillar of support, the one who's made the greatest sacrifices on my behalf. You encouraged me to take on this huge project and I truly couldn't have done it without you. I love you.

INDEX